The HERBARIST

The War Years
1940–44

A Publication of
The Herb Society of America

Printed by CreateSpace.com

THE HERB SOCIETY OF AMERICA
9019 Kirtland-Chardon Road
Kirtland, OH 44094
www.herbsociety.org

*Originally published 1940-44 by
The Herb Society of America.
All rights reserved. No part of this book may
be reproduced in any form without written
permission from The Herb Society of America.*

ISBN: 978-0-9979242-2-0

Dedicated to the Herb Growers of the Home Front.

FOREWORD

Founded in 1933, The Herb Society of America was less than a decade old when the Second World War began in Europe. Their members, like everyone else, had endured the Great Depression of the Thirties, but affecting them on a more personal level were the unexpected deaths of two of their seven founders, Mrs. Florence Bratenahl and Mrs. Harriet Brown. Such a blow might have weakened another organization, but members remained stalwart as they prepared to meet the challenges of a new decade.

In September 1939, Britain, France, Australia, New Zealand, and Canada declared war on Germany. Americans, although not yet officially engaged in the conflict, felt its effects immediately. German submarines, known as U-boats, began attacking commercial ships in the Atlantic. As a result, culinary and medicinal herbs, long imported from Europe, would be difficult, if not impossible, to obtain. The European sage supply was cut off, and drug companies predicted there would be a real shortage of digitalis.

Enterprising truck farmers, commercial growers, and drug companies wondered if these herbs could be grown profitably in America. Sage grew well in the New England climate; digitalis could be found in the wilds of the Pacific Northwest. It was also being grown in the Midwest, leaving some growers to wonder if it could be cultivated in New England.

Having little or no information, they turned to The Herb Society of America, where their requests were referred to The Society's

Commercial Research and Publication Committee, which was chaired by Mrs. Adeline Cole, one of the organization's founders.

Years later, Mrs. Priscilla Lord, The Society's historian, wrote that Mrs. Cole was "a sheer genius in accomplishing her goals, and was second to none in her insatiable curiosity, and in her approach to research." Chairing that committee, at this particular moment in history, was a test of her abilities, and she did not disappoint.

Mrs. Cole realized quickly that The Society's members had no experience growing the vast quantity of herbs required. They had little technical information to share about cost or yield per acre, nor did they possess a stock of seed. She began by asking members to start their own test plots, under a quarter acre, and record the results.

In December 1941, as this research was underway, America entered the war. The call to enlist was met with enthusiasm. The ensuing labor shortage made weeding and harvesting difficult for growers, but they persisted and were able to meet the nation's needs. Throughout the war, Mrs. Cole and her committee continued to correspond with growers and drug companies, sharing research and information they felt was relevant.

On the pages of the following five issues of *The Herbarist*, originally published in 1940-44, contributors offer insight into the experiments undertaken by The Society, the conclusions they reached about the importance and focus of their work, and their hopes for the future of herb growing. We hope you enjoy reading their observations from The War Years.

The HERBARIST

A Publication of

The Herb Society of America

No. 6

For Use and for Delight

BOSTON, MASSACHUSETTS

1940

The Herbarist for 1940
A Limited Edition
Written and Published by
The Herb Society of America
Price $1.00

Copies of the 1936, 1937, 1938 and 1939
Herbarists may be purchased
at $1.00 each.
(1935 is out of print)

Address

The Herb Society of America
Horticultural Hall
300 Massachusetts Avenue
Boston, Massachusetts

Copyright, 1940, By The Herb Society of America

CONTENTS

	PAGE
FRONTISPIECE: Lavender	4
Original Etching by Caroline Weir Ely	
FOREWORD	5
NATURAL FLOWER OILS . . . . . *Dr. Ernest Guenther*	6
SIXTEENTH CENTURY POMANDER BALL — ENGLISH — Illustration	14
AN EXPERIMENT IN LAVENDER PRODUCTION *Frances Thorpe*	15
THE RECOVERY OF DILL OIL . . . . *E. W. Hagmaier*	19
THE FUTURE OF HERB GROWING . *Martha Genung Stearns*	24
SAGE . . . . *E. M. Wilder*	31
TEA HERBS IN EARLY AMERICA . *Helen Noyes Webster*	34
A SIMPLE HERB DRIER . . . . . . *Arnold M. Davis*	42
OUR CONTRIBUTORS	44

LAVENDER
Original etching by Caroline Weir Ely

FOREWORD

IN every war which has affected the commerce between Europe and the western continents, America has been forced to depend largely on her home-grown crop of condiment and drug herbs. At the close of every war, the grower who has risen to the emergency has been unable to hold his market against revived foreign competition and lowered prices no matter how good his product.

In the following pages, members of the Herb Society of America, expert in their several fields, report on their experiments and experiences, discussing some phases of the problems involved in the revival of the once prosperous industry of Herb Growing in America.

NATURAL FLOWER OILS

DR. ERNEST GUENTHER

WHILE until about one hundred years ago a perfume was composed mostly of plant extracts, tinctures and perhaps a few distillates, a modern perfume is an extremely intricate mixture of many raw materials. Chemical science, plant growers' and distillers' experience, and the perfumer's art combine to create those exquisite products which we admire for their delightful and intriguing scent.

A modern perfume consists of an alcoholic solution of ingredients which can be classified into two groups:

First, a great selection of aromatic chemicals or so-called " synthetics," developed by the untiring research of generations of brilliant chemists and manufactured in the complicated apparatus of chemical factories in accordance with the most advanced processes. This branch of organic chemistry has advanced so far that it is nowadays possible to reproduce, for instance, the delightful scent of lilac flowers perfectly true to nature. It is impossible for me to go deeper into this complicated and purely chemical subject, but I would like to point out that we are still very far from reproducing all flower perfumes synthetically.

The second group of raw materials employed in perfumes consists of the natural flower oils and the so-called " essential " oils, several hundred of which are at our disposal. Essential or volatile oils are distinguished from fatty oils by the volatility and pronounced fragrance. A fatty oil is usually not fragrant and does not evaporate.

Essential oils occur in many plants and in different parts of the plants. A very simple example is the orange or the lemon, the peels of which contain numerous glands filled with essential oils. It is possible to liberate the essential oil from the cells of such fruit by simply squeezing the peel, and upon this simple principle all processes of citrus oil manufacturing are based. Other essential oils occur in leaves, for instance, oil of peppermint and oil of geranium. By crushing a leaf of such plants between the fingers one can readily determine the presence of essential oil by the scent. Other essential oils are found in the roots of plants or in the bark, as in cinnamon bark, or in the wood, as sandalwood. Those oils are usually extracted from the plant by steam distillation whereby live steam is blown into the still so that the essential oil is carried over into the condenser, reliquefied and separated.

The most delightful and most important essential oils are contained in the flowers. By extracting rose petals, jasmine flowers, orange blossoms, tuberose flowers, we obtain the so-called " natural flower oils," the production of which has become a very important industry in the South of France along the Riviera. These priceless ingredients of perfume raw materials are extremely expensive, one pound of absolute of jasmine costing about $350 and one pound of tuberose about $2,000.

Chemistry, engineering, and art have combined in an attempt to extract from delicate, fragrant blossoms their true scents, and a special industry has grown up, principally in Southern France, and more recently in Bulgaria, Egypt, Algeria and Sicily. Factories equipped with apparatus of modern technical design specialize in the manufacture of these priceless products, and research is constantly carried out on the methods of extraction, in an endeavor to further improve quality and yield of oils.

Regular essential oils are usually obtained from plant material by the simple method of distillation with steam. But the flower is usually the most delicate part of a plant, and the heat attendant on steam distillation undoubtedly exercises a deteriorating influence on the original natural oil in the flower, affecting the chemical constituents and consequently the perfume. Therefore, strictly speaking, only those oils extracted with volatile solvents or fats come under the heading " Natural Flower Oils."

The principle of extraction with volatile solvents is simple: fresh flowers are charged in specially constructed extractors, and in the cold extracted systematically, with a very carefully purified solvent, usually petroleum ether. The solvent penetrates the flowers, and dissolves the natural flower perfume together with the flower waxes present in the plant cells. This flower oil solution is subsequently pumped into an evaporator, and concentrated at a low temperature. After the solvent is completely distilled off in vacuo, the concentrated flower oil remains in the still. Thus no harmful heat is applied during the entire process, and the danger of chemical action on the delicate flower perfume is avoided.

An interesting development of recent years has been the experimentation with natural flower oils in America. Some creditable oils have been produced, and gardenia has been manufactured on a semi-commercial scale. It is to be hoped that despite the high cost of labor prevailing in the United States, native flowers which are available in profusion in certain sections of this country will eventually be utilized in the manufacture of floral products. Of course, before such a venture could be undertaken on a larger scale much experience would be required in the growing of plants and in the proper methods of extraction.

The industry of natural flower oils is attractive to the lover of the beautiful. It is most interesting to the horticulturist, the practical engineer, and to the organic chemist because the most delicate problems of biochemistry are involved. The secrets of nature, the actual processes according to which plants develop, utilize or discard flower oils, are unknown. The chapter is only opened, and the more we penetrate into the mysteries, the more fascinating and complicated the problems become. Much still remains to be done. For instance, the yield of natural flower oils may be substantially increased and the cost reduced by the proper selecting, propagating and cultivating of such plant varieties which are resistant to diseases, easy to cultivate, easy to cut, and which develop the most essential oil.

Work along the lines carried out by Luther Burbank in California should be undertaken. Perhaps some day the biochemist will succeed in developing processes of submitting flowers to the influence of certain enzymes, whereby the oil yield may be increased. There is further possibility of utilizing new solvents, or combinations of solvents, by which flower oils more true to the natural scent can be obtained. There are still many flower varieties which have never been experimented with, especially in tropical countries. New notes and scents could be developed by utilizing those exotic creations of nature. The possibilities in the industry of natural flower oils are considerable.

THE LAVENDER INDUSTRY IN SOUTHERN FRANCE

LAVENDER grows on sunny hillsides, preferably on calcareous soil. We find the true lavender (*L. vera officinalis*) in high altitudes, from 700 up to 1500 meters, distributed over mountain slopes and hills of the Departments of Drôme, Basses-Alpes, Vaucluse, and Hautes-Alpes. In lower altitudes we find the spike lavender (*L. Latifolia*). The quality of lavender changes, therefore, with the altitude. Of course, climatic conditions, humidity, temperature, atmospheric pressure, exposure to sun, etc., especially soil conditions, play an important rôle in the development of plants and oil.

Since the essential oil from plants growing in the highest altitudes shows the highest percentage of linalyl acetate, and since the spike lavender oil distilled from plants originating in the lower altitudes has almost no linalyl acetate, the quality of oil of lavender is being more and more judged by its content of linalyl acetate.

It is difficult to estimate the cost of a plantation of lavender. Everything depends on whether the lavender plantation is only a part of another agricultural enterprise of the farmer, so that the general expenses of the plantation can be included in the expenses of running the farm. A farmer and his family who devote themselves to the planting of lavender at a time when they are not busy with the harvesting of grain, olives, and other products of Southern France, can produce much cheaper than a distiller who runs a separate enterprise solely for the purpose of cultivating lavender. As a matter of fact, it appears that the cultivation of lavender is profitable only if it is a part of a general agricultural enterprise.

Although the yield of the first year may be absolutely insignificant, the plants must be cut. In the second year the cutting still represents a high cost, because of the fact that the production is very small, and it must be done very carefully, due to the necessity of preventing injury to future harvests. Since the original investment in a lavender plantation represents a considerable amount of money, a planting should last at least eight years to bring any profit which can be expected only in the fourth and succeeding years. A few years ago a great number of lavender plantations in Southern France died, to the great discouragement of the farmers, and with the result that the wild growing flowers from the higher mountain slopes had to be used for distillation. Lately the nature of the disease has been identified as *Sophronia Humerella*, Schiff., the caterpillar of a minute butterfly, and remedies have been suggested which may bring about a revival of lavender plantations in Southern France. During the last few years distillation material has consisted mainly of wild flowers.

Up to about twenty-five years ago, all the oil of lavender was distilled in migratory open-fire stills. These migratory stills were convenient, and the transition to steam stills was not made without extensive discussion and much controversy. The cost of lavender oil depends primarily on the price paid for the flowers, and secondly upon the yield of oil. The expenses involved in the distillation itself are of minor importance. The main factor here is the cost of the fuel, and coal and wood in modern lavender distilleries are usually replaced by the sun-dried plant material resulting from the distillation.

After the oil is distilled the exhausted plant material, when not used as fuel for distillation, is dried in the sun and passed through a simple device separating the flowers from the stalks. These flowers, despite the fact that their essential oil content has been removed, are sometimes sold for cheap sachets or for filling pillows. Of course, in order to obtain a normal quality of dried flowers, they should not be distilled first but separated from the stalks after cutting and drying.

The lavender oil industry of Southern France has not been in the best of condition because of overproduction, competition and adulteration of oil, which all together leaves very little profit for the growers. Furthermore, oil of lavender has found a serious competitor in Oil of Lavandin distilled from a hybrid between *Lavandula vera officinalis* and *Lavandula latifolia*. This hybrid lavandin lends itself much better to cultivation; the plantations are much less subject to diseases and give a higher yield of flowers and oil. Many farmers have, therefore, replaced their lavender plantations with lavandin plantings. The oil of lavandin distilled in the same type of stills as oil of lavender is a lower grade lavender oil and, therefore, cheaper. However, it seems to work out very nicely as a soap perfume for which it is being used in increasingly large quantities.

Oil of lavender can be produced not only in Southern France but also in other parts of the world. Successful experiments have been carried out during the last few years on Puget Sound in Washington, where several hundred pounds of oil have been distilled. The quality of this oil is very satisfactory. Other experiments on a much smaller scale have been undertaken in California and also around Salt Lake City. However, the main producing region is still Southern France which in 1938 produced about 65 tons of oil of lavender.

England produces only several hundred pounds of oil a year, but the quality of this oil is quite different from the French lavender. Experiments undertaken in Kenya, East Africa, with true French lavender completely failed, probably because of too high altitude and the absence of a blanket of snow in winter under which the plants can be dormant for a few months.

When experimenting with lavender, it should be borne in mind that growth for two or three years is not indicative of final success, which is assured only after the planting has survived for at least eight years.

NATURAL FLOWER OIL OF JASMIN

THE delightful, fragrant jasmin originated in Asia. About a thousand years ago the jasmin bush, like the orange tree, was brought to Southern Europe by the conquering Arabs and cultivated in Spain, Italy and Southern France.

To capture the delightful scent of the tiny white flowers has long been the endeavor of man; we know that the natives of India absorb jasmin flower oil with vegetable fats by some primitive form of enfleurage which is really maceration. The Western perfumers' art has found in the jasmin flower oil one of the most valuable and indispensable ingredients for creating modern perfumes.

Jasmin is cultivated on a large scale primarily around Grasse, and recently to a limited extent in Egypt, Algeria, Northern Italy and Sicily. In the region of Grasse, cultivation of the jasmin flower forms part of the individual farmer's occupation. In addition to his vegetable gardens, olive and fruit groves, he uses part of his property for raising jasmin flowers. While the French Riviera is still by far the most important producing region for natural flower oils, there is, nevertheless, a tendency to develop a similar industry in northern Africa, and especially in Sicily. In fact, Sicily has become quite important during the last few years because of suitable climatic conditions and the lower wages prevailing there than on the French Riviera. During the last ten years the Riviera has developed into a summer as well as a winter resort, and in many cases the peasants there might find it more profitable to raise vegetables and fruit for the many hotels along the Côte.

There are several varieties of jasmin (*Oleaceæ*): in Southern France, Jasminum Grandiflorum, or *Jasmin D'Espagne,* is grafted upon roots of wild jasmin, Jasminum Communis. It grows particularly well on the southern slopes of Alpes-Maritimes which are exposed to the sun and protected against north winds.

Starting a new plantation is a relatively costly enterprise, requiring quite an investment in the clearing of the ground and particularly in the construction of walled terraces necessary for good irrigation.

The jasmin flower harvest usually starts at the end of July and lasts until the end of October. The flowers of August and September are considered the best; of course quality depends entirely on weather conditions — rain, wind and cold being detrimental to the yield of oil. Picking is done every day early in the morning. It has been experimentally established that the flowers in the early morning are richest, not only in essential oil content in general, but especially in indol. From five o'clock in the morning until ten, one woman can pick 2.5 to 3 kilos of flowers. One kilo contains 10,000 jasmin flowers; the figure is lower at the beginning of the harvest and higher towards the close of the season.

The duration of a jasmin plantation ranges from fifteen to twenty years. In soil not sufficiently dry a plantation ages quickly. On the other hand, with light well-aired soil, easily drained, a jasmin plantation will last much longer. Plantations of the Comtesse De Savigny in Seillans have lasted thirty-five years. After a plantation of jasmin has died, no new jasmin can be planted in the same soil.

The absolutes of jasmin made by volatile solvents (petroleum ether), because of their considerably lower yield, are correspondingly more expensive than the absolutes obtained by the enfleurage process. Since they contain all the odoriferous principles of the living flower present at the moment of picking, these absolutes of extraction represent the highest form of natural flower oils.

Jasmin flower oils are widely used in all types of scents, not only floral but in those of Oriental character as well. To the latter they impart a delicious heaviness and a smooth roundness which is not obtainable with other ingredients. In floral types, jasmin absolutes create a certain natural note, a finishing touch, without which a composition remains crude. However, the mere addition of jasmin flower oil does not necessarily mean improvement of a compound; only in a well-balanced, harmonious base of synthetics and essential oils can jasmin develop its greatest merit of beauty.

SIXTEENTH CENTURY POMANDER BALL — ENGLISH
Courtesy of Museum of Fine Arts, Boston, Massachusetts

"This pomander or scent ball, of silver gilt, is in the form of an orange. When opened, each segment is shown to have a narrow sliding lid whereon is engraved the name of a perfume: *Cedro, Rose, Garfoli, Naransi, Viole, Moschete, Ambra, Gesmini.*" — *M. F. A. Bulletin.* October 1936.

AN EXPERIMENT IN LAVENDER PRODUCTION

FRANCES THORPE

WITH the hope of establishing, in the future, lavender culture as a minor or cottage industry in California, an initial planting of lavender seed was made in April, 1937, on the family ranch near Santa Paula, and the name of the ranch " La Promesa " — the promise — rather aptly describes the present status of the experiment. The ranch is fifteen miles from the seacoast with an approximate elevation of 500 feet and lies at the foot of mile-high coast range mountains. The climate is mild, having a usual minimum temperature in Winter of 30 degrees and a Summer maximum of 95 degrees. The soil is Yolo-silt loam. The lavender plot of less than one-half acre lies on a southwest slope and has excellent drainage. It was cleared from a virgin growth of white and purple sage — *Salvia apiana* and *Salvia leucophylla*.

My seed was of a strain of lavender of the subspecies *Lavandula Delphinensis* which in Dr. Guenther's opinion produces in France the highest grade of oil obtainable.

Transplanting of the lavender plants from lath-house to open ground began on the sunny New Year's day of January 1, 1938. The plants, set three feet apart, were planted in rows and the distance between the rows was also three feet. As the soil was virgin, no fertilizer has as yet been applied. The first year the plants made a slow growth and during the Winter months remained practically dormant. From May 1st, which is the end of the rainy season, they were irrigated and cultivated once a month until the first rains of Autumn in October. In the second Spring the plants made a much more rapid growth and by the middle of last June each hardy plant was in full, beautiful, purple bloom.

The following is the report given by Dr. A. J. Haagen-Smit of

LAVENDER PLANT, TWENTY YEARS OLD, ON AZVEDO RANCH
AT LIVINGSTON, CALIFORNIA

LAVENDER FIELD AT "LA PROMESA"

the Organic Chemistry Department at California Institute of Technology who kindly superintended the distillation of the lavender flowers in the laboratories of the Institute:

"The lavender was collected on the farm 'La Promesa.' The plants were in full bloom in the middle of June when the flowers were cut. 23 kilograms were distilled with dry steam and the oil layer was separated from the water layer.

    23 kg. lavender yielded 175 gr. of oil (0.75%)
    Refractive index $25°$ 1,4648
    Density at $15°$ 0,8855
    Ester content   39.2%
    Free acid given as tenth
    normal base per gram of oil   0,99 ml."

Based on the weight of the fresh material used, the yield of oil was about five-tenths of one per cent. The oil content was not high and this may have been due to the young stage of the plantation, as the optimum of oil output is usually found after the plants have grown for at least four or five years.

A sample of oil with analysis was sent to Fritzsche Brothers and Dr. Guenther in commenting on its quality says that the oil has a very clean odor which he considers very good and that the ester content of 39.2 per cent is good indeed, and compares favorably with good French oils.

At this time, if considering only my own limited experiment, it would seem that the cultivation of lavender in Southern California commercially would not be feasible on farm lands of high value. The labor employed, the cost of irrigation and the rather slow growth of the plants would preclude adequate profit. However, I have learned recently that if lavender plants are set in the open ground during the rainy season, irrigation is not necessary. Near Livingston, in Central California, on the ranch of Antoine Azvedo, an industrious Portuguese farmer, I have seen huge plants of English lavender — *Lavandula vera* — which have been growing, he tells me, without cultivation and without any artificial irrigation for more than twenty years. In June last, when I first saw the plants, they were a mass of bloom and Mr. Azvedo assures me they have never missed a season of producing flowers. The soil is sandy decomposed granite, not particularly fertile, and the temperature has a wide range. The plant illustrated, unfortunately not in bloom when the picture was taken, is twelve feet in diameter. The proven longevity and productiveness of the plants are very encouraging facts and with artificial irrigation eliminated, a better grade of oil should be produced. Marginal lands and parcels of small acreage, particularly when the owner and his family are also the laborers, could well be planted. On ranches of more value the irregular and uneven plats, not susceptible of easy irrigation, could be utilized. In many different sections of California there is land, inexpensive because not well thought of agriculturally, which should prove ideal for lavender culture and for producing oil of high grade. It is my intention, in the near future, to make small plantings in at least three widely separated locations. Hoping for very good results at a higher altitude, a planting will be made at an elevation of 3,000 feet in Tuolumne County near Big Oak Flat, one of the old mining towns on the Mother Lode.

The first yield of " La Promesa " oil of lavender has been used as one of the principal ingredients in a delightful toilet water made from an old formula for Eau de Cologne. As a tangible result, it is gratifying and pleasing evidence of my effort, and the delicate and refreshing fragrance is a reminder of many hours spent in lath-house and sunny field.

" But flowers distilled, though they with winter meet,
Lose but their show; their substance still lives sweet."

THE RECOVERY OF DILL OIL

E. W. HAGMAIER

SOME twelve years ago the problem of finding out something about dill oil, and its recovery, was dropped in my lap.

Up to that time I had been familiar with the imported oil for seasoning pickles, but had never given any serious thought to its constitution or manufacture.

Now my problem was to make it. The first thing was to take some of the imported oils and have a chemical examination made of them. I soon found out that so-called dill oil was a complicated combination of several oils, of different chemical constitution and characteristics. I also found that every so-called dill oil did not contain the same proportions of these different constituents.

I found that dill oil was made up principally of three main constituents; a hydrocarbon called anethene, with the formula $C_{10}H_{16}$ with a decided turpentine odor, and a boiling point of 150-155C., a second hydrocarbon called carvon with the same formula, but a boiling point of 170-175C., and having the odor of mace, also an oxidized compound called carvol with the formula $C_{10}H_{14}O$ and boiling at 225-230C. The gravity of dill oil is around .881 and the color varies from water white to a pale yellow or straw.

The next thing was to figure out a distillation set-up, since information on the subject was very scarce, we decided to pattern our method after that used in recovering oil from mint.

Two retorts, a condenser and separators were erected, and as soon as the weather permitted ten or twelve acres of seed was planted. This end of the work was entrusted to the field man for a large kraut manufacturer, as I had no experience in this end of the process.

When he said that the weed had matured, he started to harvest, and delivered the weed to the recovery plant. After the first retort was properly charged and sealed, the steam was turned on and distillation started. In a very short time the air about the still was

Dill Weed Ready for Harvest

Cutting and Binding Dill Weed

permeated with a strong dill odor, and soon a very dark oil began to separate from the water on top of the separator. Distillation was continued for about two hours and we collected about three quarts of a very dark oil with a decided dill odor, but having a very sharp after flavor.

One retort after another was charged and distilled, and the distillates collected. After each retort was exhausted, a close examination of the spent weed was made and we learned that those containing over-mature weed gave the darker oil.

Chemical examination of our recovered oil showed us that the dark color and sharp tasting constituent were an oxidation product which could be removed by refractionating. This gave us a straw-colored oil with a very good dill flavor. When compared to the imported oil we found that our oil was stronger and had a more characteristic dill weed flavor. This was the only redeeming feature of our first experiment, for financially we took a loss.

During the winter we made more experiments, and decided on changes in our distillation set-up. We made changes in the design of the separators, as we found the old ones did not recover all the oil. Changes were made in the condensing system in order to make it more efficient.

The next season we tripled our acreage and staggered the time of planting in order that we might be able to distill without getting much over-mature weed. From the changes we made we were able to increase our yield about thirty per cent. The oil was much lighter in color and had a fine odor and flavor, and was pronounced superior to the imported oil. Even with this increase in output, from a financial standpoint we still lost money.

We made further refinements in our distillation set-up, installed a mechanical method for rapid discharging of the retorts, and tried to speed up production and increase production wherever possible. Up to this time the spent weed was permitted to dry sufficiently, and then burned. This was a very smoky and smelly method of disposal, and did not give us any return. After some experimenting we found that by treating with Cyanimid, and inoculating with some fresh manure, we were able to add humus to our soil.

LOADING SPENT WEED ON TRUCK

ADDING CHEMICAL TO FACILITATE BACTERIAL DECOMPOSITION

Each year we have made little refinements on retorts, condensers, separators, and methods of handling the raw, and also the refined product. Exact records and close observation and study show us that with equal amounts of weed charged, and identical conditions, there is considerable variation in the amount of oil recovered. The only variable we can lay this to is the weed, and we are now making quite a study of the weed, experimenting with different seeds, methods of planting, fertilizing, soil conditions, and cultivation in general. This is going to take some time before we have really collected any sound, positive information.

As I said in the beginning, although I have worked with the extraction of dill oil for the past twelve years, there is still plenty to learn. This much I do know positively and that is that the venture has not been a great financial success. Even though one is able to perfect all the mechanical parts of the process, and even improve the plants, Nature's whims must also be in your favor, for on these each season depends chances for a good yield. Drought may dry out your plants, too much rain drown them out, or heavy winds and rains may lay a good stand low, thus giving a poor harvest and increasing costs. We have experienced all of these and I can assure you that the pioneer in the essential oil industry dare not have a faint heart or be easily discouraged.

In conclusion I would emphasize that, due to cheaper foreign labor, it is imperative that our domestic product be superior to the imported oils, and that it really requires large scale manufacture in order to succeed financially.

THE FUTURE OF HERB GROWING
A Hopeful Outlook for New England

MARTHA GENUNG STEARNS

THE American farmer is a cautious man. As the descendant of generations of hardworking people with a long, uphill row to hoe in order to wrest a living from difficult soil, it is natural that he should have learned to do things the hard way, and to be slow to depart from tried methods to run after innovations which may prove to be ephemeral.

He understands milk and eggs and poultry; he knows all about apples and the endless sprayings and mulchings and graftings, and knows only too well what a hail storm can do in a few minutes to a crop after slow months of ripening. He recognizes potato bugs, cutworms and army worms, and is learning new kinds of beetles; he has come to know in the past years how hard it is to sell hay, and all the things that may happen to his timber land. These things have become ingrained and have made him what he is — a cautious man about changes.

If you go to such a man and tell him about a new kind of crop which will grow in any reasonable soil with the minimum of insect pests and blights, which only needs to be sown, weeded, harvested and dried, with little fertilizer and no spraying, and give him the figures per acre for the sale of it as a sure thing, he will look at you as if you had said that a thousand dollars in silver were lying there in his field. In order to convince him, you must tell him the story more than once, with proofs; and even then, he will doubt — until his first check comes in.

The story of herbs is so old that it has been forgotten completely, or become a mere legend, a grandmother's tale. That is a very good name for it; for those New England grandmothers knew all about the herb industry. Time has marched on and left the old homely methods behind; but that does not disprove the fact that there was great good in them. The trouble lies at the door of the patent medicine makers and the searching laws which forbid any deviation from the standard packaging of drugs and foods put up commercially. An instance is that it is no longer possible for a druggist legally to make up a mixture of glycerine and rose-water to soften your hands; he can only sell you a bottle of each for you to mix yourself. The law forbids tampering with original packages and the standard contents embalmed therein.

To go back to the beginning of the story takes us into the past of a hundred years and more. Every household lived in close coöperation with the soil and every one knew a vast deal about nature's virtues. Dried herbs and seasonings were a part of every harvest, not only to liven up the plain and somewhat heavy food, but for simple household remedies and preventives. Dye plants were grown or gathered for home use. Ships sailing on long voyages stocked up with herbs in their medicine chests; and certain herbs were in demand for export. The Shaker communities flourishing in the 1850's took the lead in the cultivation of drug-plants, and it is estimated that their output of valerian oil alone brought in $10,000 annually in New Hampshire. Horehound, camomile, wormwood and many other crude drugs brought the annual income for New England soaring up over a million.

If we cared to go into the more romantic aspects of the subject and talk about the part which herbs played in daily life and economy, there is much to say. But we want to get away from the kitchen array of salads and seasonings, and from the " fingerbowl gardens " which are the present fad, and get into the fields. We want to speak about herbs on a heroic scale. It is well, therefore, to mention facts and figures, and the best way to put it clearly is to give actual examples from a modern experiment.

In 1936 an experiment was begun in New Hampshire, known as the Medicinal Herb Project, under the direction of the State Department of Agriculture, with some aid from W.P.A. funds. It was intended to revive this old industry and prove to the farmers that herbs could be a paying crop. As Mr. Andrew Felker, Commissioner of

Agriculture, said, it takes an acre to grow a ton of hay, and hay sells now at $8 a ton. As the number of animals dwindles, hay is becoming an obsolete crop; there must be some more profitable crop for an acre of land to be put to.

Investigation was made as to supply and demand, and the government reports showed that great quantities of herbs and condiments were being imported from Europe, and that these were often not of first quality. We find that in 1935 America imported 6,168,202 pounds of caraway seed for which $410,095 was paid. Caraway grows tall and luxuriant as a roadside weed in New England; what would it do with a little help and cultivation? We read that 15,578,058 pounds of pyrethrum flowers were imported at a cost of $2,041,993. Is there any reason why that two million could not have been spent at home? We pick up the information that American firms dealing in seasoning for poultry dressing have been importing large quantities of sage from Dalmatia; it is harvested in that country with a reaper, like hay, and when it arrives it is full of weeds and sticks, so that the weight shrinks considerably with cleaning, to say nothing of the labor required to process it. This does not compare favorably with the crisp gray-green of homegrown sage, which retains its color when dried and is pungent and tempting. We wonder how it is that dealers can accept the gray, powdery product from abroad which retains scarcely any odor. One more illustration has to do with a certain popular remedy for sprains and bruises put up commercially in this country, in which wormwood is a chief ingredient. During the World War, its manufacture was seriously curtailed for want of imported wormwood, and did not go forward until a crop could be grown in this country. Wormwood will grow beyond all bounds in ordinary garden soil.

Soil tests proved that New Hampshire, though small in area, has everything in the way of soil needed for the cultivation of superior products in drug-plants: altitude, fertile river valleys, woodland, even saltmarshes, which made it an ideal field for the experiment.

A couple of acres at Pembroke were planted, greenhouses and a drying shed built. Rows of plants were grown, partly for seed and partly to study for experimental purposes, but mostly to give to farmers in order to spread the knowledge of the subject more widely. Under the direction first of Mr. Frederick Baker and later of Mr. Forrest L. Kibbee, the Pembroke headquarters took a most benevolent interest in the experiments of inquiring farmers, from the beginning of their effort through to the end, for it furnished them with plants at no cost except a ten-cent charge for the flat; advised and aided in every way with the harvesting, and took the dried product from them for marketing. Every summer more converts were made; an increase, for instance, from 42 in 1938 to 72 in 1939. They had their *protégés* giving up strawberry beds and vegetable patches in order to put more space into herbs, which paid better. The growers were advised to limit themselves to a few varieties: catnip (with no medicinal market in this country but in great demand for pet-shops), sage, digitalis, pyrethrum, summer and winter savory, basil and marjoram.

The star performer has been digitalis, and its story is worth telling in detail, because in the opinion of many it is the most important of drug-plants. Digitalis, or foxglove, is the best known member of a group of plants which produce a characteristic action on the heart; they have come down to us from times of great antiquity and have been known to medicine for centuries; but the other members of the group (oleander, squills, hellebore, etc.) are really substitutes for the preëminent Digitalis Purpurea. Fuchs gave its botanical description in his herbal of 1542, and Gerard and Parkinson both mention it as an expectorant and emetic. William Withering in his treatise, "An Account of the Foxglove and Some of Its Medical Uses" (1785), says, "It has a power over the motion of the heart to a degree yet unobserved in any other medicine, and this power may be converted to salutary ends."

Digitalis is a biennial, familiar in flower gardens as an ornament for the border, with its tall spires of color. But in medicine, the leaves are the official portion of the plant. Mr. Felker planted a small test plot on his own farm in Meredith, N. H., an area of 24 x 64 feet. From 420 plants he cut 806 pounds of green leaves, which yielded 160 pounds dried. The figures per acre, based on this plot, are as follows: At the low estimate of 25 cents per pound for 7,430 pounds

Work Projects Administration

DIGITALIS PLANTS BEING GROWN IN TEST PLOT AT MEREDITH

Work Projects Administration

DIGITALIS PLANT GROWN AT MEREDITH HERB PROJECT

to an acre, the price brought in is $1,857.50. These are the sort of figures which sound like a fairy tale to the cautious New England farmer when he contrasts them with the price of hay per acre. This digitalis was treated as an annual, and the plants shown in the illustrations are all first-year plants, a few of which were allowed to grow seed.

The digitalis which I saw dried was magnificent, with beautifully clean green leaves, no waste or dust, a product superlative in appearance and testing at 50 per cent more potency than the imported product. As this drug is administered in very small doses, this amount represents a very intensive crop. I was reminded that many thousands of pounds are imported annually, America only growing one-fiftieth of what it uses.

Basil has great commercial value and is an easy annual grower. Early frosts in New Hampshire sometimes catch it unawares, but in Massachusetts it might almost yield two crops. It is cut as soon as it begins to bloom, as the tops quickly go to stem; in fact as soon as it is established, a preliminary cutting back will stimulate a thicker plant.

Out of this Pembroke experiment, two facts have emerged: the necessity for careful drying, and the imperative need of careful grading of the product, especially if grown on several different farms. The most practical way to take care of these would be by making the herb-growing industry coöperative, with a group of growers working around a center. Plenty of farmers and private growers can be found who are willing to plant their land to herbs, which will grow easily from seed and flourish in ordinary soil such as garden vegetables grow in. But there must be sound drying methods, and some fixed standard must be adhered to in the grading.

It would therefore be desirable for a group in a neighborhood to get together in the construction of a central drying shed or barn, where the different plants harvested could be uniformly treated in preparing them for market, and judged by a qualified person. The purpose of drying is to prevent the decay of the product, at a slow enough rate so that it retains its color and qualities, yet without danger of mould. The rate of drying is controlled by the temperature and amount of circulating air, and the old method was to hang the herbs up on wires in an attic or other room which is kept dark and airy. Another way is to spread them thinly and loosely on trays made of screening, or even of loosely woven fabric such as burlap. This air-drying process can be hastened by low artificial heat for a short time toward the last. When the leaves are thoroughly dry they must be packed in cartons or bales for shipping and kept from any possible dampness. The drying shed at Pembroke was somewhat primitive, owing to lack of funds; but that did not prevent excellent results.

Perhaps the initial crop should be reserved largely for seed, which would give a good start for the future, judging by the instances we have seen. In my own small experiment with coriander, the result produced was almost embarrassing, for out of one packet of seed sown in a row among the vegetables, we gathered nearly three pound coffee tins of fine clean seed. Incidentally, the 1935 report says that 618,322 pounds of coriander seed were imported at a cost of $74,574. Other herbs which are prolific yielders of seed are dill and camomile.

It has been thought that the mints are not as practical as other herbs for growing in New England, for they are bulky and it takes a great area to make very much when they are reduced to oil, which is the chief form in commerce. The New England growers would do better to grow in smaller quantities the sort of herb or drug which repays personal care, and in the harvesting and preparing of which careful handling is more desirable than mere quantity production.

Basing our judgment on the beautiful crops resulting from New Hampshire's three-year experiment, it seems absolutely certain that New England can compete most successfully with the foreign growers. And just now, as imports are cut off by war conditions abroad, we may have our great opportunity to capture the home market for American grown goods. It calls for a twofold education: first, of the local grower, in persuading him to try the new crop and abide by the simple rules for its success. And second: of the dealer, in proving to him that he can buy a superior product nearer home.

SAGE

(*Salvia Officinalis*)

E. M. WILDER

EVERY European conflict shows us how helpless we are in regard to our supply of condimental and medicinal herbs. A great move is on foot to make the United States more self-supporting and self-contained in this respect. A few experimental projects have been tried with great success. We need more education in this regard — it is well worth one's time.

Growing herbs may rehabilitate our deserted farms and help take up the slack in labor. Who knows, the herbs of tomorrow may be grown in the United States? The land, soil, and climate are within our borders. For nearly forty years the Shakers had a virtual monopoly of America's condimental and botanical drug business. Their products were shipped all over America and to foreign countries. I can remember when we ground, pressed, packaged, labeled, and distributed their herbs.

The two most important items of that time were New England Sage and Lovage Root. New England Sage enjoyed the "Grade-A" distinction for many years, and always commanded a premium price.

After the passing of the Shakers a great many fields of Sage were grown by our thrifty farmers. Gradually, however, New York brokers started to offer foreign Sage, such as Greek, Dalmatian, and Spanish, to our dealers. These new sources of supply at first seemed inconsequential, but as the brokers were anxious to make sales, our dealers were just as ready to increase their profits. Low prices on account of low-priced labor prevailed. For the most part, the first foreign Sages which were sold were unsatisfactory due to the fact that the odor and flavor, savors of Camphor and Turpentine. This may not decrease its value medicinally, but as a condiment makes a very poor substitute. In my mind that is why a great many people dislike Sage. Foreign Sage Leaves can be distinguished by their thick, short, woolly leaves.

Sage leaves and flavoring tops abound in a volatile oil. This is obtained by water distillation. The oil of Sage has been used in cheeses and certain types of condiments with little success. Mother Nature seems to hold back something delicate and subtle that the distilled oil does not contain. The natural Sagebrush or the purple Sage of the western plains have no medicinal or condimental value. The purple Sage is highly esteemed for fattening cattle — they eat the ripened tops and seeds.

The ordinary Sagebrush belongs to the Genus Artemesia, valuable only to authors and romantic song writers. Ancient English Herbals mention Sage medicinally as follows:

For dizziness in the head, drink Sage Tea sweetened to taste. Nervous people will find that Thyme and Sage used as a tea will give relief. When hair falls off, dampen it frequently with Sage Tea. An old adage proclaims, " No man need doubt the wholesomeness of Sage. It is good for the head and the brain. It quickens the senses and memory." Old-time people drank Sage Tea as a pleasing beverage. An oft-quoted line was, " How can a man die in whose garden Sage is growing? " Because of its reputed health sustaining properties, Sage has been held in the highest regard.

Our New England or American Sage is a native of Southern Europe and has been naturalized for very many years as a garden plant. Our soil, climate and manner of cultivation have so completely changed the plant that it is hardly recognizable in comparison. The flavor, color, texture and type far surpass any of the European varieties. I have had the pleasure of sitting in with foreign brokers a great many times to decide the merits of different types of Sage.

After winning the point, the question was always the same — How much can you get? The answer — Very little. Apropos of this fact, the United States imported the following amounts of foreign Sage in the years:

1936 . . . . 1,629,248 pounds
1937 2,033,505   "
1938 1,235,979   "

Noting the variation in the amount imported in 1937 and 1938 it will be very interesting to get the report for 1939.

As far as I know, in New England we have three of the first largest and best spice mills in this country. With this in mind, think what the raising of 2,000,000 pounds of Sage could mean to our New England States or even to the whole country.

Medicinal herb growing is not a " get rich quick " enterprise, but propagation of the hundred or so herbs and plants that the crude drug business depends upon. It is not only possible for the small farmer or the drug plant specialist, but it is also as profitable as staple farming when properly conducted.

American cultivation of medicinal herbs and plants is vitally necessary at the present time to prevent our entire dependence upon foreign countries for many vital medicinal requirements.

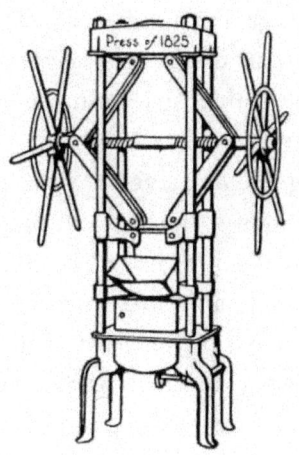
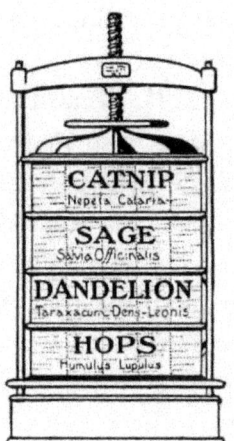

like Sage. Foreign Sage Leaves can be distinguished by their thick, short, woolly leaves.

Sage leaves and flavoring tops abound in a volatile oil. This is obtained by water distillation. The oil of Sage has been used in cheeses and certain types of condiments with little success. Mother Nature seems to hold back something delicate and subtle that the distilled oil does not contain. The natural Sagebrush or the purple Sage of the western plains have no medicinal or condimental value. The purple Sage is highly esteemed for fattening cattle — they eat the ripened tops and seeds.

The ordinary Sagebrush belongs to the Genus Artemesia, valuable only to authors and romantic song writers. Ancient English Herbals mention Sage medicinally as follows:

For dizziness in the head, drink Sage Tea sweetened to taste. Nervous people will find that Thyme and Sage used as a tea will give relief. When hair falls off, dampen it frequently with Sage Tea. An old adage proclaims, " No man need doubt the wholesomeness of Sage. It is good for the head and the brain. It quickens the senses and memory." Old-time people drank Sage Tea as a pleasing beverage. An oft-quoted line was, " How can a man die in whose garden Sage is growing? " Because of its reputed health sustaining properties, Sage has been held in the highest regard.

Our New England or American Sage is a native of Southern Europe and has been naturalized for very many years as a garden plant. Our soil, climate and manner of cultivation have so completely changed the plant that it is hardly recognizable in comparison. The flavor, color, texture and type far surpass any of the European varieties. I have had the pleasure of sitting in with foreign brokers a great many times to decide the merits of different types of Sage.

After winning the point, the question was always the same — How much can you get? The answer — Very little. Apropos of this fact, the United States imported the following amounts of foreign Sage in the years:

```
1936........1,629,248 pounds
1937........2,033,505    "
1938........1,235,979    "
```

Noting the variation in the amount imported in 1937 and 1938 it will be very interesting to get the report for 1939.

As far as I know, in New England we have three of the first largest and best spice mills in this country. With this in mind, think what the raising of 2,000,000 pounds of Sage could mean to our New England States or even to the whole country.

Medicinal herb growing is not a " get rich quick " enterprise, but propagation of the hundred or so herbs and plants that the crude drug business depends upon. It is not only possible for the small farmer or the drug plant specialist, but it is also as profitable as staple farming when properly conducted.

American cultivation of medicinal herbs and plants is vitally necessary at the present time to prevent our entire dependence upon foreign countries for many vital medicinal requirements.

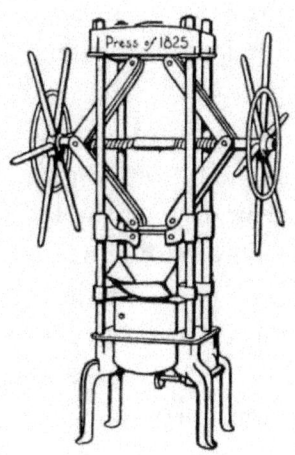

TEA HERBS IN EARLY AMERICA

HELEN NOYES WEBSTER

THE American colonist brought with him to the new country the Old World prejudice against drinking water as a beverage. Apart from light wines, ales, and strong waters, the only other source of their drinks was robs, hot drinks, teas, tisanes brewed from the herbs of the homeland. Almost immediately in this new land the women were forced to test the beneficence of new simples as substitutes in making their gentle, purifying tisanes. Sassafras, spice bush, sarsaparilla, pine buds, black birch bark, salina, or the inner layer under the bark of the spruce, Labrador tea, reindeer moss, Indian posy, wild ginger, American elder, and a score of other native herbs were quickly learned and accepted by the colonist, and herb tea was both his drink and his medicine. Whether true or not, that story of Joe Pye coming out of the woods with his arms full of boneset to cure the Pilgrims, will make me forever look with affection at the joe-pyeweed in our meadows.

The story of these herb teas has always intrigued me. From childhood there has ever been a fascination about the aromatic plants. Like all country children who play naturally, we nibbled at and made our teas of fragrant spicy plants. Through the haze of distant Maine summers drift early memories of crinkly pastures, covered with wintergreen: we ate the berries and crushed the juicy leaf tips in birch bark cups for our tea. We mixed young sweetbrier leaves with a couple of the sticky, pungent green burrs found on the new stems of the prickly bushes, and called it lemonade. We thought it all our own discovery; no one told us then that our Puritan ancestors and their English mothers knew more about herb teas than we. While the early colonist was struggling to find native beverages for the family, in England a new herb was being imported from China and becoming the fashionable drink of London. It was Charles II's Queen Catherine who substituted China tea at the court in place of

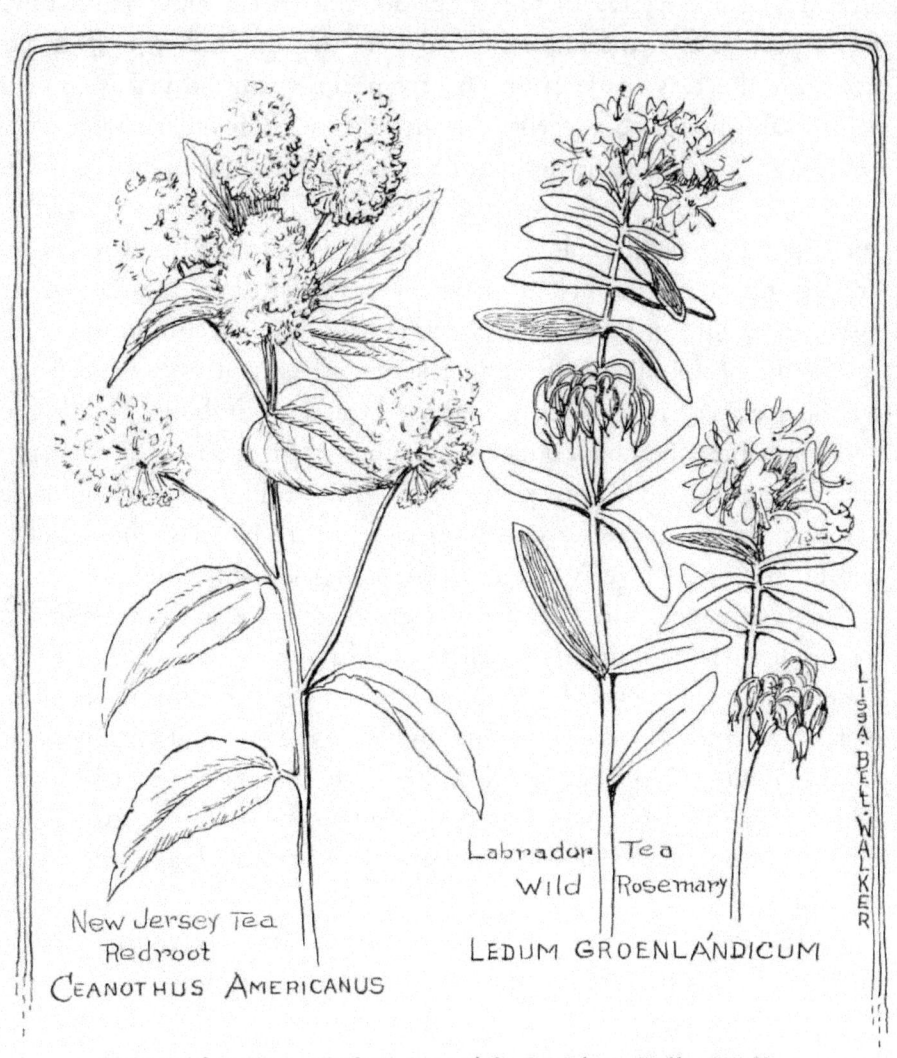

Drawn for Mrs. Webster's article by Lissa Belle Walker

ales, light wines and spirits. The colonist, ever eager to follow the fashion of the day, soon was importing this new leaf. And the practice of this China tea drinking spread like an epidemic from town to outpost. For a time it became one of the essential enjoyments of life, and the teas made from the aromatics, grown by this time in well-established herb gardens, fell into disuse. The older people alone refused to give up their herbs for the novel Oriental brew. It is said that in the history of America, China tea drinking never reached such popular heights as in the era just before the Revolution. Smuggling and attempts to grow the tea shrub here,* to avoid the heavy taxation, did not long postpone the day of rebellion.

No more foreign tea! In 1775, the fiercest patriotism was measured by the degree of relish with which herb teas were imbibed. Herb gardens came into their own once more: lemon balm and bee balm, catnip, calamint and spearmint, pennyroyal and ground ivy, chamomile, peppermint and lavender and fennel seed were brewed alone, and in combinations as cleverly tricky as those of the modern hostess.

Next to peppermint, sage was a great favorite; its tea sometimes flavored with condiments savoring of luxury, — mace, cinnamon, lemon, rum or honey. Hot sage tea sweetened with thin maple syrup is still a Vermont tradition. Short, in his classic dissertation upon teas, speaks of sage "As the only English herb that has put in its competition or rivalship with the foreign plant — Chinese tea — and indeed seems preferable. Chinese themselves preferred sage, and would trade one to four."

In the annals of the Revolution are frequent references to the common use of herb teas, and many of the wild or native plants used are called today soldiers', war or patriots' tea. Wild snow ball, or Jersey tea, and swamp tea, or Labrador tea, were invigorating and

---

*From *Boston Gazette,* 1768: " In 1768 tea made from a plant or shrub grown in pearsontown about 20 miles from Portland Maine was served to a circle of ladies and gentlemen in Newbury port, who pronounced it nearly if not quite its equal in flavor to genuine Bohe tea. So important a discovery claims attention, especially at this cricis. If we have the Plant, nothing is wanted but the process of curing it into tea of our own manufacture. If a Receipt cannot be obtained gentlemen of Curiosity and Chymical skill would render this country an eminent service if by Experiments they would try to investigate the best method of preparing its use."

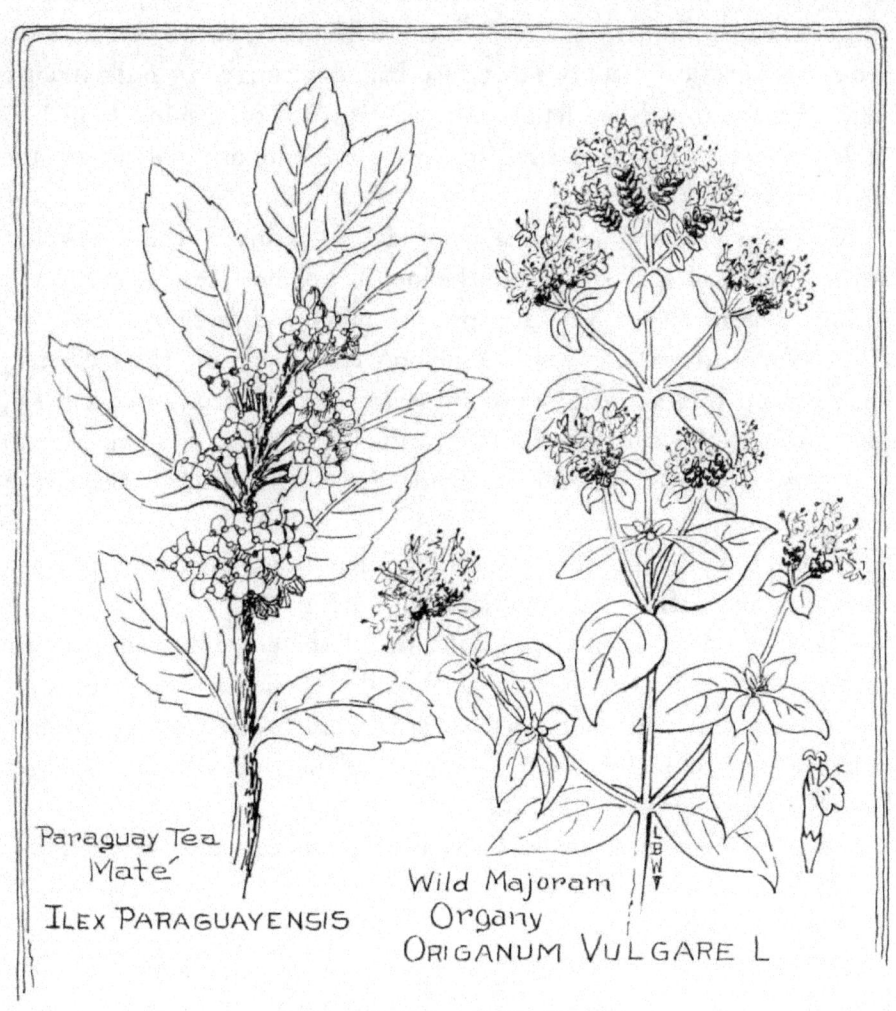

Drawn by Lissa Belle Walker

necessary tonics. At home, herbals were searched, and grand-dames' tottering memory refreshed for new brews which were sturdily dispensed at the tea tables, and which might delude the partaker to forget the abandoned store tea. Every wild plant, shrub or tree with aromatic bark, leaf, root or flower was hailed with fervor, and patriotic news sheets fanned the flame of patriotism by publishing long lists of liberty teas. England tried to save the monopoly enjoyed by the British East India Company and she lost an empire.

Almost a century later the Confederate Army Surgeon Porchat added other healthful simples to the long list of herb teas of the Revolution. Licorice root, ginseng, princes pine, and dogwood bark the Civil War soldiers knew well, and brewed and drank for medicine, courage and refreshment. Most important was a strong black brew, long used by the Virginia Redmen, called cassena or yaupon. It was a strong, powerful stimulant, made from the dried leaves of a southern holly.

Darlington, in his "Flora Cestrica," has much to commend in a very pleasant infusion of cunila, Maryland dittany.

The methods used in the making of all these brews seemed never to vary. Roots and barks were boiled till the good was out. Flowers and leaves which give up their essence were brewed in the earthen pot — a pint of boiling water to the handful of dried herb, a larger handful if the herb was green.

Today pioneer progress and travel have carried the beverage herbs far afield from their original homes, and enriched thereby the dietary of the health propagandist.

The motherly old herbalist who bought or gathered her dried herbs and dispensed from her parlor Wahoo Powder, Pulmonary Syrup, Lavender and Blood Medicine has been displaced by medical clinics and soda fountains. The catalog of a modern health centre reads like the Liberty Tea list in the *Saturday Evening Post* of 1775: wild strawberry leaves, chamomile flowers and thyme are brewed for the nervous and troubled; aromatic little herba buena from California mountains, and peppermint leaves, for the weary. Parsley tea, raw carrot and cresses with lemon and salt counteract, you are told, that lethargic indifference to living.

Pale tilleuil, from the sweet flowers of the European linden, almost as popular today as when French kings praised this digestive stimulant. Boteka is another ultra-modern tea wherein the new vitamin K is introduced through alfalfa leaves.

The calabash herb of South America is another holly whose dried leaves have for centuries made the stimulating and national drink called Yerba Maté or Paraguay tea. This, brewed in a gourd bowl, is sipped through a silver bourbillon, and so sustaining is the brew that the natives depend upon it for both food and drink for long journeys.

A collection of the plants which provided the herb teas before coffee, China tea and chocolate became national beverages was assembled at the herb festival at Hancock, N. H., in the summer of 1939. Here one could study the living plant, root, stem, leaf and bark, and taste the brews from some of them: brews pungent and spicy as well as bitter and medicinal.

PARTIAL LIST OF LIBERTY TEA HERBS AND SOME AROMATIC PLANTS KNOWN TO HAVE BEEN USED FOR HOT STIMULATING DRINKS IN EARLY AMERICA

Native herbs

American pennyroyal, *Hedeoma pulegioides,* infusion of whole plant sweet and " minty "
Anise goldenrod, *Solidago odora,* leaves taste like sweet chervil
Black spruce, *Picea nigra* ⎫ young tips and leaves and inner bark called
Red spruce, *Picea mariana* ⎭ " Saliva "
Checkerberry, wintergreen, teaberry, *Gaultheria procumbens,* evergreen plant, spicy
Dogwood, *Cornus florida,* bark slightly bitter, a tonic with sweet herbs
Hemlock, *Tsuga Canadensis,* new leaf tips steeped and sweetened with maple sugar
Jersey tea, redroot, *Ceanothus americanus,* dried leaves
Holly, *Ilex Paraguayensis,* dried leaves make the tea, " maté "
Holly cassena, *Ilex vomitoria,* dried leaves make the tea, " yaupon," called the Black drink
Indian posy, everlasting *Anaphalis margaritacea,* whole plant

Labrador tea, swamp tea, wild rosemary, Revolutionary tea, *Ledum Groenlandicum,* evergreen leaves, fresh or dried

Licorice, *Glycyrrhiza glabra,* dried root very sweet

Linden, limetree, *Tilia Americana,* flowers and bracts make the beverage tilleuil

Oswego tea, beebalm, *Monarda didyma,* leaves and flowers

Sarsaparilla, *Aralia nudicaulis,* very aromatic root

Sassafras, *Sassafras variifolia,* bark of root

Slippery elm, *Ulmus fulvus,* inner bark which is mucilaginous in spring

Sumac, *Rhus typhina,* also *Rhus glabra,* clusters of red berries which have a salty taste

Sweet birch or black birch, *Betula lenta*

Thoroughwort, boneset, *Eupatorium perfoliatum,* whole top of herb makes a bitter infusion which was popular combined with the sweet herbs

Wild bergamot, *Monarda fistulosa,* leaves dried for flavoring hot water, but little taste

Wild raspberry, Flowering raspberry, probably *Rubus odoratus,* though the dried leaves of *Rubus strigosus* and *Rubus idæus* are indicated in some accounts. The leaves and bark of the former species are commonly used today

Wild rose, *Rosa Carolina,* petals of flowers and hips

Wild strawberry, *Fragaria Virginiana,* dried leaves

Witch hazel, *Hamamelis Virginica*

Introduced herbs used for beverage in early America

Anise, *Pimpinella anisum*
Borage, *Borago officinalis*
Calamint, *Calamintha officinalis*
Caraway, *Carum carui*
Catnip, *Nepeta cataria*
Chamomile, *Matricaria chamomilla*
Dill, *Anethum graveolens*
Fennel seed, *Fœniculum officinale*
Giant Hyssop, *Agastache anetheoides*
Ground Ivy, gill-over-the-ground, *Nepeta glechoma*
Herba buena, *Micromeria chamissonis*
Lavender, *Lavandula vera*
Marjoram, *Origanum vulgare*
Pennyroyal, *Mentha pulegium*
Peppermint, *Mentha citrata var. piperita*
Saffron, *Carthamus tinctorius*
Spearmint, *Mentha spicata*
Thyme, *Thymus serpyllum*
Wild basil, basil mint, *Satureia vulgaris*

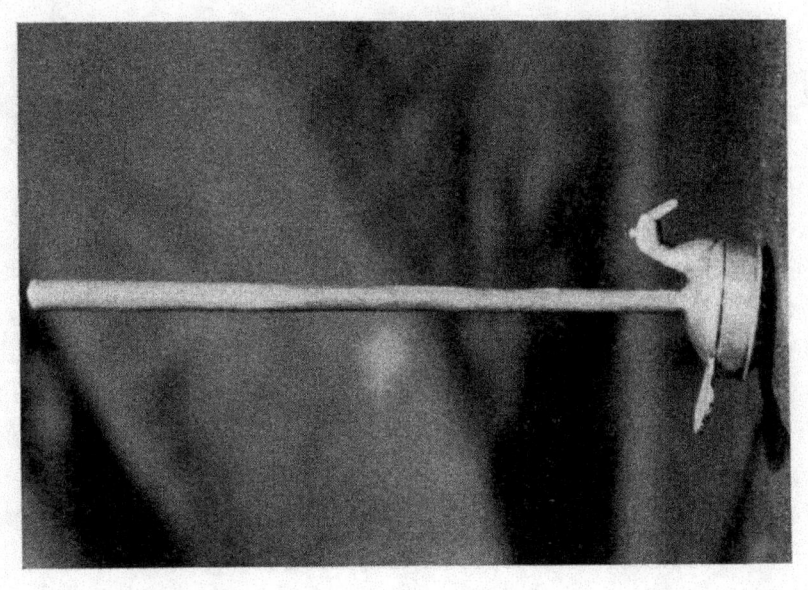
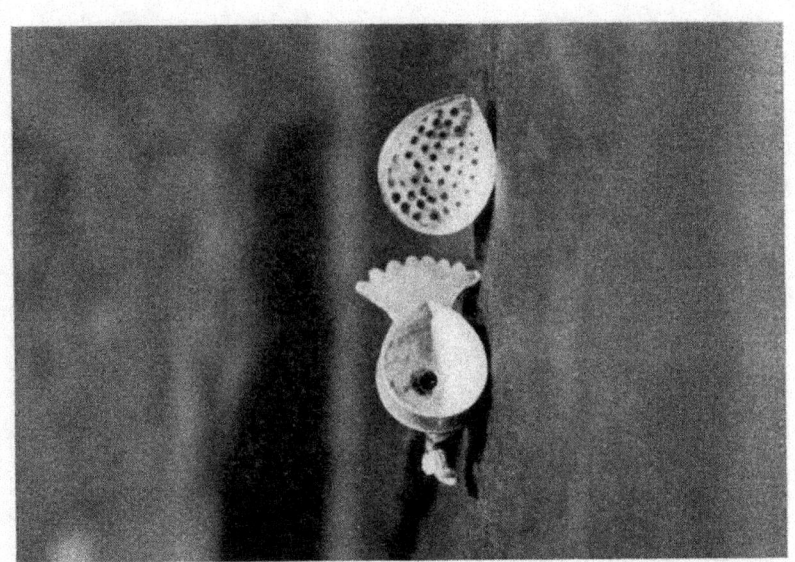

Bourbillon or Maté Tube — From Chile, South America (About 1850)
Courtesy of Mrs. Francis Dane

A SIMPLE HERB DRIER

ARNOLD M. DAVIS

THE greatest difficulty confronting the amateur grower of herbs is a simple and inexpensive method of curing his product.

The sun-drier, illustrated, is inexpensive to construct, and inexpensive to operate; the idea is not original, but has been used by beekeepers for a long time as a means of extracting honey from combs no longer valuable. The drier, made of $7/8''$ material, may be constructed by any practical carpenter. A sheet of gray or white muslin is tacked below the glass: this muslin will filter out enough of the light to preserve the color of the leaves. The disposition of the water which will result from the dehydrating of the leaves of the plant is provided by the holes bored in the side of the drier. These are $1''$ holes placed $3''$ apart on the four sides of the drier and are covered with hinged plywood drops. When the herbs are first placed in the drier all of the drops are open. As the drying process advances one or more of these slides are closed until the entire circulation of air is excluded.

To get best results with such a drier it should be turned with the sun so that in the morning it will face east and in the late afternoon it will face west. Of course, the most effective time of the day will be high noon when the sun is almost directly overhead and thus generates its greatest heat. If herbs are picked early in the morning and placed in the drier they should be completely dried by afternoon and in good condition for either permanent storage or other processing. This statement would apply to a bright sunny day in the middle of summer. In the early spring and in the late fall, when the sun's rays are not as powerful, the herbs will need a longer period to dry. This is perfectly safe, if the drops are closed at sunset, to exclude moisture. This drier is definitely for the home grower and not a commercial appliance. With a little practice it should give a superior dried herb with a minimum of effort.

HERB DRIER
SIDE VIEW
SECTION OF EDGE OF GLASS FRAME
GLASS FRAME
18"
HINGED PLYWOOD DROP
9"
36"
BLOCKS FOR TURNING
SUPPORT TABLE
PIPE IN CENTER OF BLOCKS TO FACILITATE TURNING
DES BY A M DAVIS
DRAWN BY E.S.BEAUMONT

HERB DRIER
END VIEW
24"
GLASS FRAME FITS OVER SIDE OF DRIER
1" WIRE MESH ON BOTTOM
22"
18"
34"
9"
CLEATS ON INSIDE TO SUPPORT TRAY
REAR DOOR HINGED TO ALLOW TRAY TO BE SLID IN
TRAY
SUPPORT TABLE
DES. BY A.M.DAVIS
DRAWN BY E.S.BEAUMONT

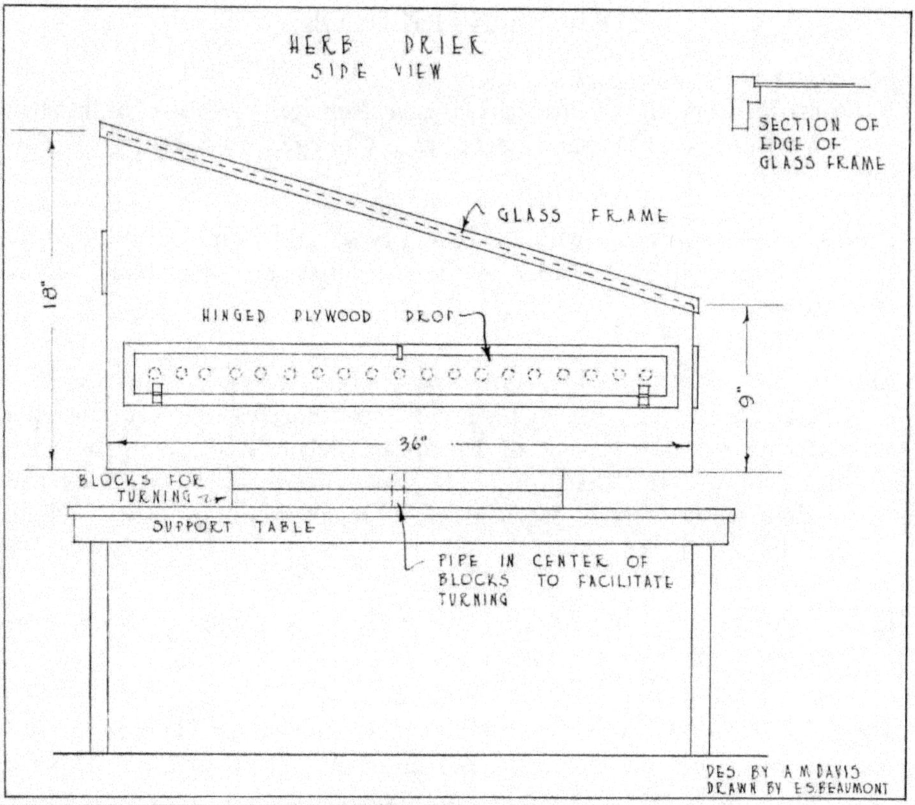

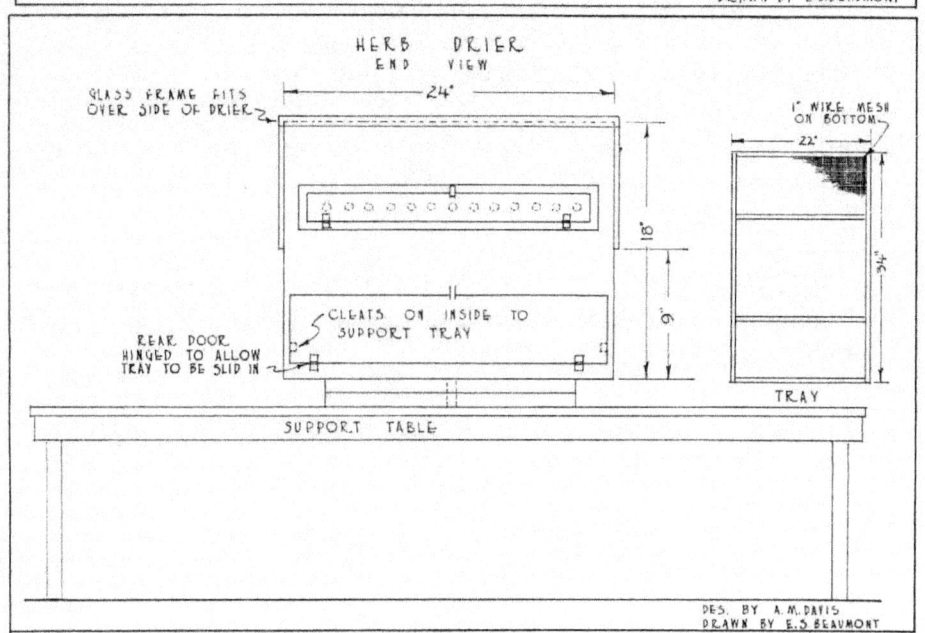

OUR CONTRIBUTORS

ARNOLD M. DAVIS. Professor Davis, Extension Professor of Horticulture at the Massachusetts State College, Amherst.

CAROLINE WEIR ELY. Mrs. G. Page Ely of Old Lyme, Connecticut, the daughter of J. Alden Weir, the artist, and herself a skillful etcher.

ERNEST GUENTHER. Dr. Guenther, chief research chemist for Fritzsche Bros., Inc., in his article summarizes the results of his private research survey of European methods for scientific data on growing and distilling. He was assisted in his work by the coöperation of the Agricultural Departments of the various countries visited.

E. W. HAGMAIER. Mr. Hagmaier, a consulting chemist, comes from Pittsburgh, Pennsylvania.

MARTHA GENUNG STEARNS. Mrs. Foster Stearns of Hancock, New Hampshire, a member of the council of the League of New Hampshire Arts and Crafts, and editor of the League's *Monthly Bulletin*. Also State Chairman of Conservation of the Federation of New Hampshire Women's Clubs.

FRANCES THORPE. Mrs. Spencer Thorpe of Los Angeles, California, Chairman of the West Coast Group of the Herb Society of America, and a successful horticulturist.

HELEN NOYES WEBSTER. Mrs. Hollis Webster of Lexington, Massachusetts, horticulturist, and author of " Herbs. How to Grow Them and How to Use Them."

E. M. WILDER. President of G. S. Cheney Co. of Boston, Massachusetts, oldest herbarists in the country.

Books for the Gourmet and the Gardener!

HERBS FOR THE KITCHEN
By IRMA GOODRICH MAZZA

The most unusual cook book of the year. Miss Mazza tells you how to transfer the subtlest flavors from the garden to the table. It's chock-full of mouth-watering recipes, covering a wide range of dishes that taste better with herbs. It's seasoned with wit, and a wealth of unusual cooking lore is thrown in for good measure. The contents include:

<table>
<tr><td>Cockle Warmers</td><td>A Dish of Meat</td></tr>
<tr><td>Herbal Salads</td><td>Some Vegetables</td></tr>
<tr><td>One-dish Meals</td><td>Spaghetti</td></tr>
<tr><td>Chicken in the Pot</td><td>Brain Food</td></tr>
<tr><td colspan="2">The Thousand Faces of Rice</td></tr>
</table>

$2.00

"If you are vitally interested in herbs and their uses, don't miss it — practical and fascinating."
— *Philadelphia Ledger*

OLD-TIME HERBS FOR NORTHERN GARDENS
By MINNIE WATSON KAMM

A reference book that's fun to read — crammed with information about the origin and history of herbs, their rôle in literature and drama, their use in medicine and cookery. 44 photographs and many drawings. $3.00

"Merits a place in the library of every herb enthusiast." — *Boston Sunday Herald*

-------- Mail This --------

LITTLE, BROWN & CO.
34 Beacon Street, Boston, Mass.

Please send me............copies of *HERBS FOR THE KITCHEN* at $2.00 a copy, and ....copies of *OLD-TIME HERBS FOR NORTHERN GARDENS* at $3.00 a copy. Remittance enclosed.

Name ....

Address ....

....

AND NOW with *more* than a score of rare illustrations from the old herbals and ancient gardening books

WITCHES' GARDEN

A bound volume of the third 12 issues of
HERB JOURNAL

LIMITED EDITION
$2.00
Postpaid in U. S. A.

Mrs. Rosetta E. Clarkson
SALT ACRES
MILFORD   CONNECTICUT

First **HERB COOK BOOK** *of its kind!*

By those well-known culinary artists, the Browns: the first *complete* salad-and-herb cook book! Over 300 recipes for all occasions, all seasons. How to grow, cook, and temptingly use all kinds of herbs. Only $1.75 at bookstores, or from J. B. Lippincott Company, Washington Square, Philadelphia, Pa.

SALADS AND HERBS

By Cora, Rose and Bob Brown

AN HERB PRIMER

by G. M. BROWN
TOPSFIELD, MASS.

New and revised edition
50 cents

Thomas Todd Company

A family of

PRINTERS

for 128 years

Printers of *The Herbarist*

14 Beacon St., Boston, Mass.

Wenham Exchange

PRESENTS

MARY CHESS
New York and London

PERFUMES -- SACHETS
TOILET WATERS
BATH LUXURIES

WENHAM   MASSACHUSETTS
Telephone: Hamilton 235-W

HOVÉ
PARFUMEUR

Perfumes of the Highest Quality

At Moderate Prices
Specializing in Flower Scents

723 Toulouse Street
"Casa Hové," near Royal Street
(Formerly at 529 Royal Street)
New Orleans, La.

John Wagner & Sons

PHILADELPHIA, PA.

Peppers — Spices — Herbs
Flavored Salts and Vinegars
Crystal Salt for Grinder
Gumbo File
Nepaul Pepper
Scotch Bonnet
Salamander Sauce
Chutneys — Teas
Seasonings

Sole Agent for Boston and Vicinity

Alice Means
45 Newbury Street, Boston
Tel. COM. 1340

DISTINCTIVE AND DELICIOUS

SOUTHERN DISHES

Home cooked and vacuum sealed in modern sanitary containers.

WHOLE BROILERS with Pecan stuffing

CHARLESTON CHICKEN PILAU

CANDIED YAMS

PECAN TEA-BREAD

and other delicacies

Send for price list

RALPH ERSKINE
Pacolet Plantation
Tryon, North Carolina

HERB CENTER
WENHAM
MASSACHUSETTS

Open June 15 to September 15
1.30–5.00 P.M.

The Herb Farm
CHESTER, NEW JERSEY
(near intersection of Routes 31 and 24)

Serves
Delicious food from May until November

Sells
Scientifically dried, home-grown Culinary Herbs

Write for folder

Visit
CHENEY'S HERB GALLERY

The most complete display of condimental and medicinal herbs in the United States. The display includes all of the dried flowers used in Pot Pourris and Floral Mixtures. Attic-tied herbs both medicinal and condimental are here shown.

Gallery is open from 9.00 a.m. to 5.00 p.m. daily. An attendant can be had by appointment.

G. S. CHENEY CO.
15 UNION STREET, BOSTON

FINE PRINTING

Programs — Stationery — Labels

Year Books

Estimates Gladly Given

THE PERKINS PRESS
Topsfield, Massachusetts

THE HERB FARM SHOP OF LONDON, LTD.

invites herb enthusiasts
to try their "yarbes and simples"

Now in America for your delectation . . . the herbs and herb preparations of this famous London house. We would like you to know these savoury things. So we offer the Culinary Set shown here . . . an introductory package of twelve different herbs. Zest for your cookery, a delight to all connoisseurs!

Culinary Set: *including black thyme, sage, basil, marjoram, savoury, omelette, mint, salad herbs, poultry stuffing, veal stuffing, mixed herbs and tarragon, complete with a chart for their use. For $1. we shall be glad to forward it to you, postpaid.*

THE HERB FARM SHOP OF LONDON, LTD., 347 FIFTH AVENUE, NEW YORK CITY

HERBS
SCENTED GERANIUMS
HERB VINEGARS

ROSES
CHOICE PERENNIALS
GROUND-COVERS

Catalogue on request

HIGHMEAD NURSERY, INC.
Dept. 9
IPSWICH, MASS.

Ye Olde Garrison House Gardens

BEDFORD, MASS.

WRITE FOR OUR LIST OF HERB PLANTS

and

SWEET-LEAVED GERANIUMS

Window Boxes of Culinary Herb Plants for Winter Use

WARREN AND LILLIAN DUTTON

HERBS

HERB PLANTS: pot-grown, easily shipped: spring, summer and fall.

DRIED HERBS: home-grown, dated, carefully prepared, single ingredients as well as our own popular blends for Salads, Omelets, Soups, Poultry Stuffing, Tomato Recipes, Sauces, etc.

HERB COOKERY: attractive Booklet, just published, with excellent Recipes for Herbs, sent on receipt of 25 cents.

HERB CATALOGUE: listing over 100 varieties, with cultural direction, etc., sent on receipt of 10 cents.

WEATHERED OAK HERB FARM, Inc.

Bradley Hills, Bethesda, Maryland

CHARLES H. MERRYMAN,
President and General Manager

FLORENCE BRATENAHL,
Secretary-Treasurer

FINEST HERB SEEDS

Get them the convenient way from your local dealer's display of FERRY'S SEEDS. Ask him to order special items for you.

FERRY'S DATED SEEDS

Ferry-Morse Seed Co.

DETROIT, MICH. *and*
SAN FRANCISCO, CAL.

HERBS

Soup bags   Sachets
Seasonings
Seeds
and
Plants

Write for Folder

THE LITTLE HOUSE
Margaret Norton
146 LEONARD STREET
ANNISQUAM   MASSACHUSETTS

HERBS

receive special attention in our new catalog — you will find a most interesting collection, most of which we have tested in our own Herb Garden to be sure of getting true types.

F. & F. NURSERIES

SPRINGFIELD, NEW JERSEY

Sweet-Scented GERANIUMS

Fifty named varieties

ALSO

Choice Herbs and rare plants

Write for descriptive list and prices

NORTH STREET GREENHOUSES

Danielson, Connecticut

A THOUSAND AMERICANS

from the author of "Gentlemen Prefer Blondes" to Henry Ford subscribe to the

COUNTRYMAN

because (as the London TIMES says) *"there is nothing like it in journalism; thought, humour, variety, all extraordinarily good."* THE POET LAUREATE goes as far as to say, *"I prefer it to any other periodical,"* while H. G. WELLS is one of nearly 1,000 Life Subscribers

"Such a success," said the HERALD TRIBUNE; *"unfailingly interesting,"* said the NATION ANITA LOOS sent with her own subscription, one for ALDOUS HUXLEY, and one for PROFESSOR HUBBLE, astronomer, declaring that this unique quarterly was *"almost as good as a holiday"* and *"gives Americans a fresh viewpoint."* It is not we but an American who writes *"America has nothing to compare with it"*

384 Pages	13th Year	22,000 Sales

Old customs of English rural life, humours and humanities, intimacies and realities, with scores of beautiful Illustrations you can see nowhere else, and delightful authoritative writing on Gardens, Birds, and Wild Life, endear it to every member of an American family who has visited, or hopes to visit, the Old Country

☞ Book-thick and book-high, THE COUNTRYMAN (which comes to you 4 times a year) is *of permanent value* — you will never throw it away. It is evidence of its high standard that it excludes 18 kinds of advertising

★★★ Just sample it by posting a dollar note to our address, Idbury Manor, near Kingham, Oxfordshire—which is why it is a really rural periodical. We'll send you, post free, two specimen copies of different dates and you'll know England as you've never known it before

---

Second Printing

Herbs

How to Grow Them and How to Use Them

By HELEN NOYES WEBSTER

Complete — Practical — Low-Priced

Here you will find famous plans of herb gardens; lists for planting period gardens and for herb families; the herbs to use in modern gardens; valuable information about the uses of herbs; and of course complete cultural information. Written by one of the country's leading authorities, it will make it easy to have an herb garden that will be a delight to you and the envy of your friends.

160 pages - - - 36 illustrations, Octavo only, $1.00. Postpaid in U. S.

Make checks payable to

HORTICULTURE, Horticultural Hall, Boston, Mass.

The HERBARIST

*A·Publication of
The Herb Society of America*

No. 7

For Use and for Delight

BOSTON, MASSACHUSETTS

1941

Copyright, 1941, By The Herb Society of America

CONTENTS

	PAGE
FRONTISPIECE: Pot Marigold — Calendula officinalis . . . Original Etching by Caroline Weir Ely	4
CALENDULA OFFICINALIS . . . . . *Marjorie Gibbon*	5
BELLADONNA . . . . *Heber W. Youngken*	7
MEDICINE PRACTICES OF THE INDIANS OF SOUTHERN NEW ENGLAND . . . . . . *Janet G. B. MacCurdy*	16
Gladys Tantaquidgeon	17
WREATHS AND GARLANDS . . . . *Theresa Cunningham*	22
ANNATTO . . . . *Elizabeth Kay*	28
THE RED SQUILL . . . . *B. Y. Morrison*	34
THE HERB GARDEN AT THE HARVARD BOTANIC GARDEN *E. D. Merrill*	36
NOTES	38

Pot Marigold — Calendula officinalis
Original etching by Caroline Weir Ely

CALENDULA OFFICINALIS

(*A note on the frontispiece*)

MARJORIE GIBBON

CALENDULA, " the little hour glass," has its official name from the Greek Kalends, " because it is to be seen in floure in the Kalends almost of every monthe," and it is undoubtedly one of the earliest plants known to the medicine man. Originating in the Canary Islands and along the Mediterranean shores, the Calendulas spread generally over Europe and across to England. Many names, grave and gay, were acquired as it journeyed over the world. In Italy it became *Fioridi ogni mese;* in Holland, Dodoens wrote of it as " St. Johan's Blum " and added that it was " unknown in shoppes as many good herbes be." The French are concerned to call it *" Soucis,"* while Germans term it grimly *" Todtenblumen."* In England, its name had a more cheerful significance—"Husbandman's Dyall," "Sunnes Bride," " Golds," a lovely name, and after being ascribed to the Virgin Mary, " Mary's Gold," until finally combining the lowly with the high, we call it the Pot Marigold, a homely, friendly flower as it brightens a corner of the modern herb garden.

The plant soon strayed from the " Apothecarie's " to the " Dame's Garden." The temptation is irresistible to suggest a Marigold Meal for a compleat and courageous hostess. The dinner begins with mutton broth, and " none," says Gerard, " are well made without Marigold petals, and Marigold buns with golden yellow butter." Next, the main dish of " good fat beef, garnished with a few Marygold flowers . . . and serve up with sippets." The proper vegetable to go with this will be the " buds before they be floured. Boiled and eaten with butter . . . they are exceeding pleasant." Then a salad decorated with the blossoms, " for Marigolds *should* be present at the last rites of the crab that meets its end in a salad, for all to gaze upon and not to eat." Accompany this with a Farmhouse Marigold

Cheese. "Mix the new milk of seven cows with the cream from the milk of seven more cows.... Add to this three or four handfuls of Marigolds bruised a little...." Top off with a "Tart of Marygold, Primrose or Cowslips" and wash down with Marigold wine, "very golden and pleasant."

If this dinner of herbs fails to induce the proverbial contentment, why, *similia, similibus curantur* — just take a potion of the petals pounded in vinegar for "they strengthen the heart exceedingly and are very expulsive."

Superstition has given place to science, salves in commonplace containers have replaced plaisters and unguents in gally-pots; electuaries and potions are simply doses, and possets merely drinks of a sort, but the Calendula, "vivid, pungent, strong," continues today for the benefit of the "compleat woman" or her man its healing functions. In the flourishing herb shops in England an infusion of Calendula is sold as an internal medicament for varicose veins and measles, and it is also used in many ointments and washes for skin affections. In America, its use is confined to cerates and lotions, chiefly for its styptic qualities.

Yet, most of all, we prize it, not "for Ladies' Closets and their Stillalories," but for its charming contrast with the many grays in our herb gardens, and to cut and bring indoors to brighten a dreary day with its golden sunshine and so best to "cheer the heart."

BELLADONNA

HEBER W. YOUNGKEN

THE interdependence of nations is never more obvious than during a major war such as is now progressing in Europe. Already, we in America have felt its repercussions in the rising prices of many of our imported materials, none the least of which have been a considerable number of foreign drugs. One of the most valuable of these is Belladonna, importations of which into this country abruptly ceased last July.

Fortunately, while the getting was good, some of the American crude drug dealers obtained sufficient supplies of Belladonna leaves and root from abroad to take care of the country's medical needs for some months to come. Judging, however, from the small portions of Fluidextract of Belladonna now being allotted retail pharmacists by pharmaceutical manufacturing houses and the soaring prices of the drug, its preparations and derivatives, an acute shortage is foreseen before the close of 1941, unless growers in this country can produce sufficient to take care of the situation.

The entire plant of *Atropa Belladonna* Linné excepting the thick portions of its stem is recognized in the present United States Pharmacopœia under two separate monographs, namely, Belladonna Root and Belladonna Leaf. The latter consists of the dried leaves and flowering or fruiting tops of the plant, in fact, the whole overground plant excepting stems exceeding 10 mm. in diameter, not more than 3% of the latter being permissible.

Plant. *Atropa Belladonna* Linné, commonly known as Deadly Nightshade, Dwale and Black Cherry, is a perennial bushy herb native to central and southern Europe and northern Asia Minor and naturalized in the United States. It was named *Atropa* from Atropos,

BELLADONE

Port de la plante au 1/5 de grandeur naturelle
A. *Inflorescence, de gr. nat.*
B. *Fruit à maturité, avec le calice persistant, de gr. nat.*

Reproduced from "Revue Horticole," No. 14, July, 1909

one of the three Fates fabled to cut the thread of life, and *Belladonna* from the It. *bella,* beautiful, and *donna,* lady, from the use of its fruits by Italian ladies for dilating the pupils of their eyes, thus improving their appearance.

The Belladonna plant produces a root system consisting of a dense cluster of fleshy conical roots and a crown (rhizome) from which arises one or more dichotomously branched stems bearing numerous dark green leaves and later, flowers and fruits. The leaves are alternate below and in pairs above, one leaf of the pair being larger than the other. They are petiolate with a broadly ovate to ovate blade possessing an entire or nearly entire margin, an acute apex and tapering base. The flowers are mostly solitary but occasionally in axillary groups of 2 or 3 which come off between the pairs of leaves. Each flower consists of a deeply 5-cleft calyx with triangular-acuminate lobes, a tubular-campanulate corolla with 5 shallow, blunt, spreading or recurved lobes which is dull reddish purple tinged with pale green in the lower part, 5 epipetalous stamens shorter than the corolla, a bicarpellate pistil with exserted style and capitate stigma. The fruit is a fleshy, globular, depressed, black, 2-celled berry, umbilicate at its summit and with a persistent calyx. All parts of the plant are poisonous.

Old roots of well-established plants attain a length of up to a meter and a thickness at their summit of up to 5 cm. The plants develop a many headed rhizome in age from which a number of stems arise attaining a length of 1 to 2 meters.

History. Belladonna was probably known to Dioscorides, who described its dark flowers and rounded, black fruits, alluding to the plant as "Strychnon manikon." The *Grand Herbier,* published in Paris about 1504, refers to it as "Solanum furiale," a name given it by Saladinus of Ascoli in his *Compendium aromatariorum* of 1488. The old Germans of the middle ages are recorded as having employed a salve made from the juice of the plant. The toxic properties of the plant are stated to have been known to Leonhard Fuchs, a German physician and botanist, in 1542. To Matthiolus is attributed the introduction of the name Belladonna from the use of the juice of the berries by the Italian ladies in dilating their pupils. The Venetians and other Europeans used an aqueous distillate of the plant in the middle ages as a poisonous cosmetic.

Bauhin in his *Pinax theatri botanici* (1623) calls the plant " *Solanum melanokerasos* " from which the long used English synonym " Black Cherry " was derived. Conrad Gesner named the plant *Solanum lethale* and prepared a medicinal syrup from the juice of its berries. Linnaeus in his *Species Plantarum* (1753) named it *Atropa Belladonna*.

It was not until the 18th century that Belladonna received much attention by the medical botanists. One of the earliest articles on its medical botany was written by B. Sicelinus (Jena, 1724) and entitled " Diatribe botanica-medica de Belladonna sive Solano furioso." This was followed by publications by Oettinger (De Belladonna, Hal. 1739) and by Plaz (De Atropa Belladonna, Leipsig, 1776). The first Pharmacopœias to adopt Belladonna were the Würtemberg Pharmacopœia of 1771 which recognized it under " Herba Belladonna " and the Swiss Pharmacopœia of 1771 which recognized Belladonna Leaves. The London Pharmacopœia of 1809 and the United States Pharmacopœia of 1820 contained monographs on Belladonna Leaves. Belladonna Root first became official in the U. S. P. of 1860, following its commendation by Peter Squire, a London pharmacist, who prepared a tincture from it which was employed as an anodyne in the treatment of neuralgia. Both root and leaf and top drugs have since been recognized by the U. S. P. From the root an official fluidextract is prepared which enters into Belladonna Liniment which is official in the National Formulary. Belladonna Leaf U. S. P. enters into Extract of Belladonna and Tincture of Belladonna of the Pharmacopœia. Extract of Belladonna Root enters into Belladonna Plaster U. S. P. Extract of Belladonna Leaf enters into Belladonna Ointment U. S. P. and into the following National Formulary preparations: Pills of Aloin, Strychnine and Belladonna, Pills of Aloin, Strychnine, Belladonna and Cascara, Pills of Aloin, Strychnine, Belladonna and Ipecac and Compound Pills of Cascara. From Belladonna the alkaloids atropine, hyoscyamine and scopolamine are obtained.

ATROPA BELLADONNA
Deadly Nightshade

Uses. Belladonna has long been used in medicine as an anodyne, to prevent the griping of irritant cathartics, to relax overcontracted smooth muscle, as an antiasthmatic, mydriatic and for various other exigencies requiring the depression of the peripheral nervous system. It is used to diminish the secretions including the saliva, mucus, sweat, etc. It will not diminish the lacteal secretion, nor the urine, bile or ordinary pancreatic secretion. Its action is mainly due to its alkaloidal constituents. Preparations of Belladonna Root have been used effectively within recent years in the treatment of post-encephalitic Parkinsonism. Atropine or its sulfate are mainly employed to diminish secretion, to check excessive vagus activity, to stimulate the circulation, to relax overcontracted smooth muscle in asthma, spastic constipation, spasmodic dysmenorrhea, biliary and renal colic, etc., in the treatment of poisoning by various depressants like opium and chloral, etc. In ophthalmology atropine is used for the purpose of dilating the pupil, in paralyzing the muscles of accommodation, and in inflammatory conditions of the eye, as iritis and keratitis. Scopolamine is used in the form of its official hydrobromide mainly for its sedative action in acute maniacal excitement, delirium tremens and tetanus, in relieving the tremor of paralysis agitans, in Parkinsonism, and to enhance the hypnotic effect of morphine.

The Growth and Cultivation of Belladonna. Belladonna grows wild in waste ground and stony places throughout scattered areas of central and southern Europe, southwestern Asia and Algeria. It has been cultivated successfully in England, Hungary, Germany, Yugoslavia, Russia, the Balkans, France, and in many sections of the United States, especially in New Jersey, Pennsylvania, District of Columbia, Minnesota, Michigan, Indiana and California.

It appears to thrive best in deeply ploughed, moist, well-drained loam containing lime. It may be propagated from cuttings of young shoots rooted in moist sand, from whole roots, by division of crowns made early in the spring, or as is most frequently the practice, from seed. One ounce of seed is sufficient for planting an acre.

The seed should be sown thinly in pots or well-drained boxes in a cool greenhouse in winter. It germinates very slowly and irregularly.

Usually, as has been previously reported by Haynes and Newcomb, a small part of the seed germinates in 2 to 3 weeks and the remainder in 4 to 5 weeks. Increasing the humidity hastens germination during the second and third weeks but is apt to introduce damping off fungi, as shown by Koch. The young seedlings should be transferred to pots or flats in March or April to strengthen their roots. When sufficiently strong, the seedlings should be set out in the field, about 3 feet apart in each direction. The cultivator should be used to free the soil of too many weeds. During hot weather shallow cultivation is recommended. In colder parts of the country it is necessary to remove the roots from the soil during the fall and replant in the spring. In parts of the country which experience long periods of drought it is necessary to employ artificial irrigation. Cultivated Belladonna is sometimes low in alkaloidal yield. This can often be attributed to deficiency or excess of nutrients or to a want of equilibrium among the nutritive elements, especially nitrogen, phosphoric acid and potash. Deficiency in these three elements lowers the alkaloidal yield. A suitable fertilizer for the soil in which Belladonna is to be grown is one containing 4% nitrogen, 8% phosphoric acid and 4% potash. About 500 to 600 pounds per acre of the aforementioned fertilizer or from 10 to 15 tons per acre of stable manure are recommended for impoverished soil in which Belladonna is to be grown.

Harvesting. The leaves and tops should be gathered while the plants are in flower or fruit and before the leaves have turned yellow. Two crops of leaves can be gathered from first year plants and from two to four cuttings may be taken from second year plants. They should be kept in the shade and dried quickly by artificial heat, preferably in trays with wire bottoms. It is best to start drying with a moderate heat, gradually increase to 160 or 180° F. and then gradually decrease. Leaves left in an imperfectly dried state deteriorate and emit ammonia. After drying the leaves should be stored in a dry place, preferably in moisture proof containers.

Belladonna roots may be gathered beginning with the third year in autumn. They are usually ploughed from the ground after harvesting the aerial portion of the plant, then washed to remove soil and cut into segments and rapidly dried. The larger roots are split lengthwise to prevent molding before drying.

During the previous world war, in 1918, the U. S. Dept. of Agriculture reported 273 acres of Belladonna were harvested in the United States, the total production of leaves and tops being about 83 tons with an average of 600 pounds per acre. From 136 acres, 11 tons of roots were reported harvested, an average of 164 pounds per acre.

That Belladonna of high alkaloidal yield can be grown in the United

Courtesy of Eli Lilly & Co.

HARVESTING BELLADONNA
Drug Farms, Eli Lilly & Co., Indianapolis, Ind.

States has been proven by the investigations of Arny, Bornemann, Kilmer, Koch, Sievers and others.

Belladonna plants are susceptible to attacks of insects, particularly aphids and the Colorado potato beetle. Nicotine sulfate and soap (soap plus ¾ pt. nicotine sulfate to 100 gals. of water) has proven effective in destroying aphids. A weak solution of lead arsenate has proven effective in protecting mature plants against the potato beetle, but pyrethrum or rotenone sprays should be found safer.

Following the Treaty of Versailles and the return of temporary peace to Europe, production of Belladonna in this country dwindled owing to competition with the lower priced imported drug. Today, there is need for insuring this country's future supply of this valuable drug during the war and the reconstruction period in Europe to follow by a program of properly supervised and regulated cultivation.

Department of Materia Medica,
Massachusetts College of Pharmacy, Boston.

Jan. 1941.

MEDICINE PRACTICES OF THE INDIANS OF SOUTHERN NEW ENGLAND

JANET G. B. MAC CURDY

IN the lives of the early New England Colonists an important part was played by the Mohegan Indians. The English settlers were indebted to them not only for military assistance against hostile tribes but also for knowledge of the uses of native plants for food.

While the Mohegans have long been celebrated in literature their culture, characteristic of a large area of southern New England, has been neglected until recently. This culture might have disappeared but for the fact that the Mohegans have maintained a close society, retaining basic elements of tribal customs; indeed, their own language was spoken by older members of the group well into this century.

In his Journal (II, 380-81, 1645), John Winthrop Jr. mentions " Tantiquieson, a Moheague captain " under Uncas. It is of special interest that a descendant of this same captain has collected and published a list of some seventy plants used for food or medicine by her tribe (Dr. Gladys Tantaquidgeon, 43rd Annual Report of the Bureau of American Ethnology, pp. 264-274, 1925-26). Since receiving her Ph.D. degree from the University of Pennsylvania, Miss Tantaquidgeon has been connected with the Indian Arts and Crafts Board, a position which enables her to continue her studies of the uses of plants among the Plains Indians. The Herb Society of America is fortunate in securing from Dr. Tantaquidgeon the following paper for publication.

IN our back yards, along shaded country roads, and in certain remote places in the forests, one may still find species of plants that were known to and used by our Indian ancestors for medicinal purposes and for food. It is interesting to the student of Indian life to note that the use of many of these plants has persisted among members of the remnant groups in New England and it is not uncommon to find certain older members of these groups resorting to the use of simple herb remedies in case of illness.

Knowledge of the use of plants for curative purposes was acquired in a number of different ways. Usually an individual became aware of supernatural power through a dream-vision. There were certain men and women who could effect cures without the aid of herbs, and others who relied on herbs in connection with their curative practices. It is quite generally believed that persons born with a caul or " veil " may become powerful practitioners. Also the " seventh son of a seventh son " or the " seventh daughter of a seventh daughter " has supernatural power. Among the members of the Gay Head and Mashpee groups in Massachusetts it is believed that a female deity, " Granny Squannit," controls the plants and that in earlier times medicine men and women offered food to " Granny " in return for which she guided them to places where they might find certain rare plants. An old Algonkian legend tells how many, many years ago the uses of plants were revealed to animals and man by a bear.

This knowledge was considered as personal property and persons possessed of power to heal the sick either through magical practices without the use of herbs, or those effecting cures with the use of herbs, were held in high esteem by members of the tribe. The fame of certain men and women spread from tribe to tribe and I have recorded several accounts of itinerant " doctors " who within the memory of certain older members of the tribes had visited from place to place healing the sick.

It was believed that sickness was caused by evil spirits or foreign matter or bodies getting into the body of the afflicted one. The most powerful practitioners treated their patients by performing certain magical rites in order to exorcise the spirits or to " take out the sickness." Others employed decoctions and poultices of herbs in connection with their magical practices. Another group of " doctors " used only herbal remedies in effecting cures. There were secret cures and charms known only to their owners and there were a large number of simple remedies which were known to more than one practitioner. In early times the sweat bath was important and was prescribed as a purification rite for participants in connection with certain religious observances. It was also effective in the treatment of " old peoples' disease " (rheumatism).

A number of informants stated that some of the plants that were used by our people are no longer to be found. This they say was caused by the coming of White man after which certain supernatural beings and rare plants disappeared because they could not exist where civilization had crept in. Therefore, supernatural beings and rare plants could only exist in the clean forests and rocky ledges where White man had not penetrated. So it became necessary for the " doctors " to seek the guidance of " Granny Squannit " when they desired some of the rare plants.

Simple remedies using only a single plant or part of a plant were most commonly used. These were usually administered in the form of a decoction or poultice. I have, however, seen my Grandmother use the roots, leaves, flowers, barks, from a dozen plants and shrubs in making a medicine which our people regarded as an excellent spring tonic " to purify your blood."

Entire plants were tied in bundles and hung up to dry. When needed the dry leaves, blossoms or stems were broken or pulverized and the amount to be used placed in cold or hot water and steeped. Sometimes the mixture was boiled for a long time.

In gathering plants it was important not to take more than the person expected to use. In most Algonkian tribes it was customary for the gatherer to offer a small amount of tobacco to the spirit of the plant. This was done by digging a small hole toward the east side of the plant and placing the tobacco in the hole. The first plant of a species sought by the " doctor " is not picked but he leaves the offering and then walks on. Presently, so said my informants, he sees a number of plants of the desired species and takes what he needs.

Plants to be used for medicine should not be picked during Dog Days. There are certain plants which " should not be touched by September sun."

Roots and other fetishes used in preparing love charms and some of the secret cures were kept in bundles and very seldom did a practitioner disclose the contents of such a bundle. Certain medicine men and women passed on their knowledge to younger members of their families who were sincerely interested in carrying on the work of healing. This knowledge and certain personal fetishes or charms were only given to individuals " who would honor them and do good with their power."

It is said that practitioners observed very carefully certain rules in connection with preparing remedies. For example, in preparing alder (*alnus incana*) for an emetic, the bark should be scraped upward or toward the person preparing the medicine. If for a laxative, the bark is scraped downward or away from the person. In using water from a running stream the same rule is applied. Dipped with the current the remedy would act as a laxative. Against the current, it acted as an emetic.

In preparing a decoction if the liquid seemed to look cloudy it was regarded as an unfavorable sign. If the liquid was clear, it was taken as a sign that the " doctor " would be able to effect a cure.

In preparing these notes I have chosen only the more commonly used plants.

With the passing of the men and women who used their power for the healing of the sick with the aid of herbs, much has been lost concerning the use of plants. This information was gathered while in the field studying actual specimens of plants and discussing their medicinal properties with native informants.

BLOODROOT (*sanguinaria canadensis* L.) important either singly or with other plants as a blood purifier. The root exudes a reddish liquid which is used as a dye. It was used by certain tribes as a love charm.

BONESET (*eupatorium perfoliatum*) tea was administered for colds and stomach disorders. A decoction of the leaves and stems was administered "hot at night and cold in the morning." Many individuals believed boneset tea to be a cure-all and kept a pot of the brew during the winter months so that all members of the family could take occasional sips of it either to cure certain ailments or as a preventive measure.

MOTHERWORT (*leonurus cardiaca*) tea was regarded as a cure-all for diseases peculiar to women.

COMMON PLANTAIN (*plantago major* L.) which is found in most dooryards makes an excellent poultice for swellings and wounds. The smooth side of the leaf if placed on the swelling or wound tends to act as a healing agent. If it is desirable to draw out the swelling or soreness, the rough side of the leaf is placed against the skin.

Young shoots of SASSAFRAS (*sassafras officinale*) were placed in water and allowed to stand in the sun for several hours and the glutinous substance which formed used for sore eyes. The root, leaves and bark were used in a tonic with other plants.

The leaves of BURDOCK (*arctium minus* L.), GRAPE (*vitis cordifolia*), WILD MUSTARD (*erysimum cheiranthoides* L.), leaves used singly make an excellent poultice for pain or swellings. The leaves of the plant are crushed and applied to the parts affected.

CALAMUS (*acorus calamus*) root has great curative power. Used singly or with other roots it has "warming properties." Only a very small part of the root is used in making a decoction because of its strength. A small piece of the root carried in the pocket is said to ward off disease.

CATNIP (*nepeta cateria*) tea was given to infants for colic.

MULLEIN (*verbascum thapsus*) leaves and root were made into a remedy for coughs and colds. The leaves were smoked to relieve asthmatic conditions.

WILD CHERRY (*prunus serotina*) bark is steeped and the liquid drunk for colds.

WHITE OAK (*quercus alba*) bark is also used in making a remedy for coughs.

WHITE PINE (*pinus strubus* L.) bark and sap are used for coughs and colds.

In using bark from trees and shrubs it is always the inner bark that is taken and always from the east side of the tree or " the side nearest the sun."

DANDELION (*taraxacum officinale*) plant and root serves as a medicine and also for food. The root is used in a tonic with other roots and plants. The small plants are gathered and cooked as greens in the spring.

WORMWOOD (*artemisia absinthium* L.) as the name implies was used as a vermifuge.

PEARLY EVERLASTING (*margaritacea* L.) is used for coughs and colds.

RED CEDAR (*juniperus virginiana* L.) is the sacred wood. It is used for ceremonial objects. The branches were used in the sweat bath for ceremonial purification.

Our people say that " in the spring animals and man need the green things to eat." Even now the following plants are gathered and cooked either in salted water or with meat.

DANDELION (*taraxacum officinale*).

MILKWEED (*asclepias syriaca*).

DOCK (*rumex crispus*).

PLANTAIN (*plantain major*).

COWSLIP (*caltha palustris*).

NETTLE (*urtica gracillis*).

POKE (*phytolacca decandra*) or SNAKEROOT (*aristolochia serpentaria*).

WILD MUSTARD (*erysimum cheiranthoides*).

GLADYS TANTAQUIDGEON
Field Assistant, Indian Arts and Crafts Board

WREATHS AND GARLANDS

THERESA CUNNINGHAM

THE making of wreaths, garlands and chaplets is an ancient custom symbolizing many phases of life, the uses of which can be traced back to 1000 B. C. in Egypt. References to wreaths and garlands can be found in all nations of antiquity, Chinese, Medes, Persians, Chaldeans, Hebrews and many others. Wreaths of flowers were used on occasions of sacrifice, to convey honors, and in garlands as table decorations, the latter being considered a fine art by the early Egyptians. They were of such importance to these people that when the Court traveled it was as necessary for the servants to procure wreaths for adornment as loaves of bread for food. Love of flowers was a strong characteristic of these people.

Stepping several centuries forward, we read in Homer's Iliad the description of the shield of Achilles as decorated with pictures of dancing women wearing beautiful crowns of leaves and gold. In 600 B. C., Cato, in his treatise on gardens, says, " They should be planted and enriched with such herbs as might bring forth flowers for coronets and garlands." And Josephus has recorded the use of crowns of flowers in the time of Moses.

The ancient Hebrews acquired their love of floral ornament from the Persians, and the Greeks carried the taste home from the Eastern wars to the various Athenian cities, and thence to Rome. This later became the center of a floral cult so widespread that the Government was obliged to keep it under strict supervision. The Temple of Bona Dea, where their celebrations took place, was also a kind of herbarium where women dispensed herbs. The date of this temple is not known, but that of the Goddess Flora was built in 238 B. C.

From this time through the first centuries of Christianity the making of wreaths, garlands and chaplets became a great art requiring considerable mythological knowledge, and care was taken to apply the correct significance to each. The honors which they conveyed

GOLD OLIVE WREATH FROM MYTILENE
Greek. 4th Century B. C.
Formerly in the Von Nelidow Collection

GOLD BAY WREATH — Modern

were eagerly sought. Warriors fought for the civic crown of oak leaves;* poets coveted the chaplet of ivy and statesmen their laurels; Cæsar's crown was of Alexandrian laurel,† the better to conceal his embarrassing baldness by its fuller leafage. As an added distinction to the honors of these crowns, laymen were required on penalty of arrest to go bareheaded except on specified occasions. When the Roman legions returned from the wars, their generals wore the most coveted of military honors, the "Crown Obsidional" made from the grasses, reeds and wild flowers gathered from the battlefields: this crown was bestowed by the grateful soldiers on their victorious leaders.

At the height of Roman civilization these floral decorations became not only a matter of taste, but of fashion, and there was great rivalry as to their beauty and cost. In Athens a quarter of the market place was devoted to the trade and called the "Wreath market."

The base of the Roman wreath was strips of linden bark, into which they wove the flowers. These wreaths, garlands and chaplets had five definite uses: sacrificial, honorary, nuptial, convivial, and for festival. Henbane, vervain and rue for the priests and the altars; oak, olive, pine, parsley, palm, poplar and laurel for the victors; myrtle, rosemary, hawthorn and orange blossoms for the bride; daffodils and poppies for funeral wreaths, and for festivity, roses and the fragrant wild thyme. Public buildings and private homes were decked with garlands; chaplets were for personal adornment. Honorary chaplets were the prizes in the great games — the Olympian crown was of wild olive; the Pythian of laurel or palm; the Nemean of parsley; the Isthmian of pine. At the Palestra where the young men were trained as athletes the prizes were poplar wreaths, associated with Hercules.

For several centuries after Christ, lavish use of floral ornament continued among the Greeks and Romans, until the counsellors of the Christian Church decreed this practice a pagan manifestation and

---

* Montesquier claims that it was with two or three hundred oak leaves that Rome conquered the world.

† Alexandrian laurel. *Ruscus racemosus.* "Though the stalks are flexible enough to wreath easily, and the leaves resemble those on ancient busts, yet the fruit being terminal does not agree nearly so well with the fruit represented on the crowns on these busts as that of the *Laurus nobilis.*" — *Arboretum et Fruticetum Britannicum,* J. C. Loudon, Vol. 4.

FRAGON À GRAPPES

RUSCUS RACEMOSUS
Alexandrian Laurel

forbade the hanging of garlands and their uses for personal adornment. Thus the extravagance heretofore displayed decreased, never again to attain such magnificence. However, the early Christians soon realized the importance of giving the traditional festivals, so dear to pagan hearts, a Christian significance, and by a slow transition the flowers changed their symbolism to suit the legends of the saints. Lilies, sacred to Venus, were now dedicated to the Virgin; daffodils and vinca came to signify purity and virginity instead of the shortness of life as in the time of Horace.

Five hundred years after the foundation of Rome, the cult of Flora spread to England in the form of May Day celebrations, and decoration for festive occasions again took the form of wreaths.

Flowers were felt to be an emblem of beauty, and their quick fading made it natural to use them as tributes to the dead. In fifteenth century England it was the custom to have girls carry garlands composed of sweet scented herbs and flowers to be hung on the inner walls of the church, in memory of the deceased. By 1707 this practice was carried to such an extreme that the walls were dusty with dried garlands, so again after twelve centuries we find the church forbidding their use.

These floral forms during the later centuries have in turn been adapted to the beliefs and customs of the period. In the nineteenth century we find many ceremonies where wreaths and garlands play an essential part. Whatever its beliefs and customs, the human race has kept alive an inherent love for floral decoration as an expression of its strongest emotions.

"Ladies in a Garden, Making Garlands"
From an early 14th Century MS. British Museum

ANNATTO

(*Bixa Orellana*)

ELIZABETH KAY

AS AN HERBARIST who migrates to Florida each winter, my thoughts tend more and more to become concentrated on the tropical herbs — an interesting category which includes the spices and many plants that have played a part in the history of man. A curious sense of achievement and triumph steals through one's veins when one surveys a clove, allspice, nutmeg or camphor tree of one's " very own."

Probably due to the sheep-like quality (or banality) of the average human, few of these spices and flavoring herbs have been cultivated in Florida as yet. Instead, when each new home-owner has planted hibiscus and oleander just like his neighbor's, he settles back, content with himself.

It is true that some of the spice plants are quite tender, requiring a consistently tropical temperature for their flowering and fruiting. Our occasional " cold spells " discourage both the plants and those who planted them. However, almost all recover! The planters recover their optimism and the plants produce new leaves or, if they were more seriously damaged, come up from the root again. Eventually many of the plants seem to become slightly more hardy and able to ignore the northerly winds.

One of the flavoring herbs which is interesting and easily grown is the *Bixa Orellana*. This is an ornamental plant worthy of place in any garden. Its deep crimson pods are enchanting in arrangements of either living or dried plant material. Or, if one is a practical rather than an esthetic gardener, the Annatto may be grown for its uses.

Bixa Orellana originated in tropical America and the West Indies, but has spread throughout the tropical world. For years it has been a commercial crop in India, Ceylon and the East Indies, as well as in South America and the West Indies. Formerly 40 tons were imported annually through the port of Hamburg alone, and 80 tons went to England each year. However, now that aniline dyes have replaced vegetable dyes, the use of Annatto is restricted almost entirely to food and salves except among the Indians of its native habitat.

Dr. David Fairchild tells us that the scientific name Bixa was derived from the word Bicha, the name given to the plant by the Darien Indians of Panama. They have used the coloring matter from time immemorial to decorate their bodies, partly for adornment but also to afford relief from mosquitoes and other insects. (From this use as adornment comes also its more modern name of "Lipstick Plant.") The specific name Orellana was given in honor of Francisco Orellano, the discoverer of the Amazon. Other names in various parts of tropical America are, Arucu, Arnotta, Anotto, Anatto, Achiote, Achote — the last two names being of Aztec origin. In India it is also " Roucou," and in continental Europe it has commonly been known as Orlean.

This quick-growing plant, which is easily propagated from seed, becomes a large shrub or even a small tree in some localities. It thrives from sea-level to about 3,000 feet, requires no especial care and produces a crop the third year. When planted as an ornamental, it is wise to prune it well to promote the growth of new flowers.

The family — *Bixaceæ* — consists of a single genus and species. However, there are different varieties known, some having white flowers and some pink. The flowers have five sepals, five petals, numerous free stamens and a long style terminating in a two-lobed stigma. The fruit develops as a globose or ovoid capsule or pod from a half to an inch and a half long. The seed pod is reddish in color, covered with prickles. It contains numerous round seeds surrounded with the valuable orange-red pulp.

The wood of *Bixa Orellana* is a pinkish yellow, quite porous and soft. The inner bark (bast) contains a tough fiber from which twine is sometimes made. A gum, similar to gum arabic, is obtained from the branches.

As one studies descriptions of the plant written by botanists in various parts of the world, it is interesting to note the difference in the height and growth reported. Along the Gold Coast of Africa it is " a medium-sized, thick-growing shrub with flowers large, pink and very beautiful." From Venezuela, Professor Pittier reports it as a small tree, with flower petals white or rose. In the West Indies it only grows from ten to twelve feet tall while in Panama it is known to become thirty feet in height. There, as well as in Venezuela, the flowers may be pink or white. In Ceylon two or three varieties occur differing chiefly in the shape and color of the fruit which varies from oblong or pointed to circular, and may be either crimson or green. In India it grows " to ten feet " and bears " toward the end of the rains, in great profusion, remarkably beautiful flowers resembling large peach-blossoms."

Notwithstanding the charm of the terminal panicles of flowers and the density of the heart-shaped foliage, it is not for its appearance that *Bixa Orellana* has been cultivated during the centuries. The bloom has been allowed to wither untouched, for its chief value has been as the precursor of the seed pods which would follow.

When the seeds mature, the pod becomes dry and splits open, scattering the seeds. However, whether we wish them for beauty or utilitarian purposes, the pods are cut from the bush before the seeds have dropped. These clusters of ruddy, red-brown pods are delightfully decorative and will last for months. Within those which have opened, one can glimpse the brilliant seeds.

The uses of Annatto are many. Mrs. Nebel, who has known the plant in Puerto Rico (where it is called Achiote), writes of a culinary use which is new to many of us. She recommends that we marinate the seeds in our salad oil and promises that we will enjoy the rich flavor which emanates from them. The seeds should be strained from the liquid before it is served. Mrs. Nebel assures us that there is no danger from the alkaloidal content of the seeds and I am glad to add my reassurance to hers. Annatto coloring matter has been known for centuries as absolutely harmless. As it sometimes contains the crushed seeds as well as the pulp surrounding them, the seeds cannot contain a dangerous amount of alkaloid or the coloring matter would not be allowed in dairy products today.*

Several methods of preparing Annatto are described. The simplest is that of stirring the seeds in water until the pulp covering the seeds has dissolved in the water. Then the water is evaporated. The red coloring matter which remains contains substances known as " bixin " and " orellin."

A more scientific method which is used to purify the product, requires that it be treated for two days with chloroform. The chloroform is then driven off and the residue (Bixin) is crystallized. The chemical formula is $C_{28}H_{34}O_5$. For any of our readers desiring a fuller analysis, we recommend " Rohstoffe des Pflanzenreiches " by Dr. Julius von Wiesner — a book which should be found in any large library. Due to the one-time importance of *Bixa Orellana* in the dye industry, a lengthy and scientific account is given in this German encyclopedia of horticulture.

A third method directs us to take all the interior of the pod and " knead " it together. Then allow it to ferment for ten to fourteen days, by which time the fermentation will be complete. The fluid derived in this way is pressed through a cloth-lined sieve and allowed

---

* Extract from a letter received from Mrs. Nebel, December 23, 1940, as to Achiote: Dr. McCay at Cornell (Animal Nutrition) is now beginning some work on the seeds of Achiote. There has been a good deal of work done in Puerto Rico which shows that they are exceedingly high in Vitamin A. In fact there is a Vitamin A product now being put on the market which is made of the outer covering of the Achiote seeds. A letter from Mr. Lee says that any amount can be obtained for culinary use at $6.00 for 100 lbs. In a short time a series of recipes for its use could be worked up and published along with the name of some group of people from whom it might be purchased.

to settle. The clear liquid is separated from the sediment, put in a copper kettle and gently warmed until it slowly thickens. When it assumes a firm consistency it is packed for shipment as a paste or further dried for shipment in cake form. The East Indian Annatto shipped to Europe from Bengal is generally in dry form and has been considered the best in quality. Much of that shipped from South America has come from French Cayenne to Bordeaux, and has been known commercially as the " Spanish " Orlean (or Annatto). Depending upon the method of preparation, it arrives either as a soft paste, in cake form or as a powder. The color is a bright red-brown and the odor reminds one of fresh beet juice. Older Annatto at times has the unpleasant smell of ammonia.

The percentage of coloring matter varies. The variety from Cayenne has only 5% ash and for dyeing has double the potency of ordinary varieties which may have as high as 10% ash.

The uses of Annatto are quite extensive. Paul C. Standley tells us that the pulp surrounding the seeds is used medicinally, as a remedy for cutaneous diseases. It is also applied on burns to prevent the formation of scars.

The most widely known use is, however, as a coloring agent. Being harmless, Annatto is extensively used to tint butter and cheese. It enriches the color of chocolate, particularly the cheaper grades. Rice, soups, salves and plasters are also among the list of products which sometimes assume a warmer hue due to this comparatively unknown American plant.

As we have already stated, in former times Annatto was widely used as a dye for fabrics — wool, cotton or silk. Its antiquity as a coloring agent for both food and fabric is proved by findings in ancient graves in Peru. Today, however, only the natives employ it as a dye. One reason for its failure to compete with modern dyes is that it is not completely color-fast. Fabrics dyed with Annatto do not fade when washed, but are not able to keep their full color when exposed to strong sunlight. In defense of our little red seeds, let us hasten to add that few indeed are the colors of today which can truthfully claim greater permanence!

Surely it seems that the long and honorable history of *Bixa Orellana* entitles it to a place in South Florida gardens and its pods to a place in our decorative arrangements. Also, let us heed the plea that we use the seeds in our salads and otherwise experiment with this intriguing early American which was an old inhabitant when Columbus first landed in the West Indies.

BOOKS CONSULTED

Title	Author
The Indian Amateur Gardener, 2d Ed.	Landolicus
Firminger's Manual of Gardening	H. St. John Jackson
Flora of the British West Indian Islands	A. H. R. Grisebach
The Standard Cyclopedia of Horticulture, Vol. 1	L. H. Bailey
Contributions from the United States National Herbarium (Flora of the Panama Canal Zone)	Paul C. Standley
Tropical Gardening and Planting	H. F. Macmillan
Plants of the Gold Coast	F. R. Irvine
Manual de las Plantas Usuales de Venezuela	H. Pittier
Rohstoffe des Pflanzenreiches	Dr. Julius von Wiesner
Die Pflanzen Welt	Warburg
Plant World in Florida	Henry Nehrling
The Treasury of Botany	John Lindley and Thos. Moore

THE RED SQUILL

B. Y. MORRISON

THE Red Squill has an ancient and more or less honorable history as a medicinal plant. Its value is its use in a preparation of rat poisons which are extremely effective against rats but harmless to other animals. The plant comes from Mediterranean regions where it is indigenous. Due to the war the supply is uncertain. Therefore a study of the plant seems in order to determine the possibilities of its cultivation in this country should necessity arise. A plague of rats has always been an aftermath of war and the humble Squill may assume an importance it has not known hitherto.

Our species, *Urginea maritima* (L.) Baker, is sometimes called Sea-onion,* and the bulbs are described as growing only half immersed in the sandy soil near the sea, preferring not only sandy soil but hilly locations. They are collected in August, the outer scales removed, the bulbs cut transversely into slices, dried and packed for shipment. These slices are brittle when perfectly dry, odorless and possessed alone of bitterness, without the acrimony.

As sent to the American market the bulbs arrive dried and partly cut apart. The intermediate scales alone are active. There are two kinds of scales — white and red. The first comes from Spain, the latter from Italy. The color of the dried cuticle is either yellowish-white or brownish-red. When the bulbs are received alive and fresh they are usually large, rather rough and coarse looking on account of the rough outer coats that are often dried and scarred. The plant is interesting also in that it oftentimes produces bulblets within the bulb on the surface of the scales which make up the bulb proper.

Stocks of live plants seem to be rare in this country. So far, little has been done in the way of extensive experiments in cultivation, although a small stock has been developed by one grower in Seattle.

* Youngken in *The Textbook of Pharmacognosy.*

SCILLA MARITIMA

THE HERB GARDEN
AT THE
HARVARD BOTANIC GARDEN
CAMBRIDGE, MASSACHUSETTS

Planted and maintained by the New England Group of the
Herb Society of America

THE Botanic Garden in Cambridge, established in 1807, has the distinction of being not only the oldest botanical unit belonging to Harvard University, but is also the oldest botanic garden in America that has remained in continuous operation. Those established earlier in Philadelphia and New York were discontinued.

In May, 1937, through my suggestion to the Herb Society of America, 1,400 square feet of ground on the upper level was set aside for an herb garden, with the agreement that reasonable care would be provided by the regular staff, but all development would be sponsored by the Society. In October, the evergreen hedge was planted. The following year, the brick retaining wall was constructed, paths were laid out, and plantings made. The garden has now taken its more or less permanent form, and is serving a distinctly useful purpose.

Our aim has been to show how a properly landscaped herb garden might be constructed, and to demonstrate the type of plant adaptable to New England conditions. The garden is an attractive addition to a small but historically important spot, and its installation has well justified itself.

E. D. MERRILL,
Administrator Botanical Collections of Harvard University

THE HERB GARDEN AT THE HARVARD BOTANIC GARDEN, CAMBRIDGE, MASS.

NOTES

FURTHER RESEARCH makes it necessary to minimize some of the optimistic findings of the profitable growing of commercial Digitalis as reported in a previous *Herbarist*. Fantastic profits cannot be looked for nor acreage yields accurately figured from test plots. A war shortage should bring home to the United States the importance of establishing a supply of cultivated medicinal herbs. We should insure for the future a reliable source of supply not only for medicinal herbs but also for those used in condiments. The Herb Society of America is continuing to accumulate all possible reliable information in hopes that some basic plan may be worked out to stabilize a situation which is dominated by both labor costs and marketing conditions; otherwise wasted effort of capital and labor, soil and seed, will result.

DAVID FAIRCHILD, an honorary member of the Herb Society of America, has returned from a search for trees, vines and shrubs adaptable to the difficult climate of Florida. He collected seeds for the most part, some 450 varieties of ornamentals, 30 of them palms new to this area. These have been planted in his experimental garden at Coconut Grove, Florida.

EXTRACTS FROM A LETTER FROM DR. EDGAR ANDERSON: "In one garden of an Italian colony of Venetian emigrants at Rosati, Missouri, we found several ancient pollarded stumps of *Salix vitellina*, once grown for tying up the grape vines in the spring, although the younger generation now uses bind twine. These trees are the largest I have seen in Missouri. In the last ten years they have been planted extensively in Missouri as a bank covering on new soil, particularly near bridges. It has done very well and is most attractive in the winter landscape. When I saw the old trees in the Italian colony, I wondered if it might have been from there that it first came into use in this state."

MRS. FOSTER STEARNS of Hancock, N. H., has sent us the following letter from Charles Upson Clark,* Professor Emeritus, City College, New York, the discoverer of the Badianus Manuscript:

"Delving in archives is a fascinating pursuit; and when in 1929 I was invited by the Smithsonian Institution to explore European collections for unpublished documents illustrating the Aztec, Maya, Inca and other American Indian civilizations, on the Dawes Foundation, I accepted gladly. Probably to their surprise, I began this investigation at Rome; but I reasoned that three of the finest Aztec MSS. in existence had come to light there, and I knew from long previous experience that the Vatican and other Roman libraries were inadequately catalogued.

"At the Vatican I began with the latest addition, the Barberini collection, which had no catalogue, only a manuscript inventory; and I was at once rewarded, for under the heading 'Indies' I found two items which proved to be of value. The first was our present volume, modestly entitled in Latin, 'A Booklet on the Medicinal Plants of the Indians.' The inventory did not mention that it was illustrated; and you can imagine my excitement when I opened the little volume and all those charming aquarelles burst upon my vision. I carried it at once to Mgr. (now Cardinal) Mercati, then Prefect of the Library; we compared it with the known early works on Mexican botany and soon ascertained that it was unknown and unpublished, although Librarian Gabrieli of the Corsini collection had run down a copy of it in the Windsor Library in England, and was at that moment preparing an article on it for publication. Gabrieli brought photographs of the Windsor MS. to us for comparison; these photographs showed that the copyist had been inaccurate — I at once noticed that he

---

* From *Who's Who in America*, Vol. 20 (Excerpt): Charles Upson Clark has been Asst. Professor of Latin at Yale, Director School of Classical Studies at the American Academy at Rome, lectured in U. S. for Italian Government, was guest of Rumanian Govt. for several years during research; Research Investigator in Europe for Smithsonian Institution, Fellow of the Royal Historical Society and the American Geographical Society, and Mediæval Academy; Commander of the Crown of Italy — extensive writings and travels; has just returned from two years of lecture trips at Genoa, Bucharest, Constantza, etc.

had put five petals instead of six in one flower, and that he had omitted various plants altogether — and the priority of the Vatican MS. was demonstrated. With their usual liberality, the Vatican authorities waived their right to an exclusive publication of any entire MS., and this handsome volume is the result.

"The other MS., an anonymous 'Compendium and Description of the West Indies' of 1629 in Spanish, proved much more of an enigma; but investigation finally disclosed that it was the famous lost itinerary of Spanish America by the Carmelite friar Vázques de Espinosa, about which León Pinelo (who had apparently seen this identical MS.) had written that it was the most valuable account of the New World yet composed. Thanks again to the Smithsonian Institution, I have been enabled to translate this huge and interesting volume, and we hope that it will see the light this year.

"These two works are only samples of what lie hidden in archives; I am convinced that any competent investigator with ample funds and time at his disposal may hope to unearth much of what we consider lost, and cast further light on these mysterious and fascinating early civilizations."

MRS. IRENE HOFFMANN'S PURPOSE in writing another cookbook was to bring back to this country the fine art of cooking, by giving to the cooks of today a means of recapturing the creative impulse. For some years Mrs. Hoffmann has been the president of the Berkshire Garden Center and the inspiration of its herb garden. The book of herb cookery has a wide range. The recipes are eminently practical. There are no freaks of tansy pudding or marigold pie. Instead there are simple directions for seasoning with herbs which can give to the usual American dishes an added flavor.

The Herbarist for 1941
A Limited Edition
Written and Published by
The Herb Society of America
Price $1.00

Copies of the 1936, 1937, 1938, 1939 and 1940 Herbarists may be purchased at $1.00 each.
(1935 is out of print)

Address
The Herb Society of America
Horticultural Hall
300 Massachusetts Avenue
Boston, Massachusetts

The Herb Farm
CHESTER, NEW JERSEY
(near intersection of Routes 31 and 24)

Serves
Delicious food from May until November

Sells
Scientifically dried, home-grown Culinary Herbs

Write for folder

WENHAM EXCHANGE
sents **MARY CHESS** *of New York and London*
PERFUMES and BATH PREPARATIONS
WENHAM   MASSACHUSETTS
Telephone: Hamilton 235-W

BERKSHIRE
GARDEN CENTER

Stockbridge, Massachusetts

ANNOUNCES

The Book of Herb Cookery

By

Irene Botsford Hoffmann
(Mrs. Bernhard Hoffmann)

$2.50

The Book of Herb Cookery
BY
IRENE BOTSFORD HOFFMANN

With the right touch of herb flavoring, a salad will become a work of art; jellies will be inspired; cheese and egg dishes will take on a spicy difference. Though the actual herb taste may be artfully hidden, it can make the most ordinary, drab vegetable palatable; meats will lose their monotony. Here are hundreds of excellent recipes for every type of dish, giving explicit directions on what herbs to use and how to use them well. $2.50

HOUGHTON MIFFLIN COMPANY

A book about old-time New England

Homespun & Blue
by
MARTHA GENUNG STEARNS

Scribner . . . $3.50

at all book stores

The handwork of our ancestors, their nature-designs and nature-colors

---

First HERB COOK BOOK *of its kind!*

By those well-known culinary artists, the Browns: the first *complete* salad-and-herb cook book! Over 300 recipes for all occasions, all seasons. How to grow, cook, and temptingly use all kinds of herbs. Only $1.75 at bookstores, or from J. B. Lippincott Company, Washington Square, Philadelphia, Pa.

SALADS AND HERBS

By Cora, Rose and Bob Brown

Mrs. Rosetta E. Clarkson's books:

MAGIC GARDENS

A Modern Chronicle of Herbs and Savory Seeds

369 pp.   60 ill. $3.00

GREEN ENCHANTMENT

The Magic Spell of Gardens

328 pp.   60 ill. $3.00

These are MACMILLAN books
On sale at all good book stores everywhere

For autographed copies send to
HERB LOVERS BOOK CLUB
Salt Acres   Milford, Conn.

BEAUTY HERBARIUM

NEW YORK   30 Rockefeller Plaza   NEW YORK
Tel. Ci7-1995

HERBAL FACE JELLY
Made entirely of Herbs and Honey
HERBAL PACKS
For super-cleansing of difficult skin
HERBAL INFUSIONS
An aromatic steam bath for the face
HERB TEAS FOR BEAUTY
Aids to Beauty by soothing the nerves.

Write for Folder

Second Printing

Herbs

How to Grow Them and How to Use Them

By HELEN NOYES WEBSTER

Complete — Practical — Low-Priced

Here you will find famous plans of herb gardens; lists for planting period gardens and for herb families; the herbs to use in modern gardens; valuable information about the uses of herbs; and of course complete cultural information. Written by one of the country's leading authorities, it will make it easy to have an herb garden that will be a delight to you and the envy of your friends.

160 pages - - - 36 illustrations, Octavo only, $1.00.   Postpaid in U. S.
Make checks payable to

HORTICULTURE, Horticultural Hall, Boston, Mass.

John Wagner & Sons

PHILADELPHIA, PA.

Peppers — Spices — Herbs
Flavored Salts and Vinegars
Crystal Salt for Grinder
Gumbo Filé
Nepaul Pepper
Scotch Bonnet
Salamander Sauce
Chutneys — Teas
Seasonings

Sole Agent for Boston and Vicinity

Alice Means

45 Newbury Street, Boston

Tel. COM. 1340

HOVÉ
PARFUMEUR

RUE DE TOULOUSE 723
NOUVELLE ORLÉANS

Invites You to Visit
CASA HOVÉ

HOVÉ . . . housed in the mansion built in 1797 for a Spanish Grandee, with Patio and period rooms open to visitors from 10 A.M. to 5 P.M., excepting Sundays.

HOVÉ . . . in whose laboratory are created the flower perfumes, as desired today by modern women as by those of the romantic Old South.

HOVÉ . . . creator also of the individual blend for the individual personality.

Sachet Powders and Vetivert Root

FINE PRINTING

Programs — Stationery — Labels

Year Books

Estimates Gladly Given

THE PERKINS PRESS
Topsfield, Massachusetts

Thomas Todd Company

A Family of
PRINTERS
for 130 years

Printers of *The Herbarist*

14 BEACON STREET
BOSTON, MASSACHUSETTS

FINEST HERB SEEDS

Get them the convenient way from your local dealer's display of FERRY'S SEEDS. Ask him to order special items for you.

FERRY'S DATED SEEDS

Ferry-Morse Seed Co.

DETROIT, MICH. *and*
SAN FRANCISCO, CAL.

HERBS

You will find a most interesting collection listed in our catalog. Most of these have been tested in our own Herb Garden to be sure of getting true types.

F. & F. NURSERIES

Springfield, N. J.

Tressglo Makes Faded, Graying Hair Richer in Tone . . . Look Younger

TRESSGLO — new 9-herb rinse contains no chemicals — comes from the garden to answer these three vital needs of your hair.

1. Tones faded, graying or streaked hair so that it appears richer in color, younger, more lustrous.
2. Improves ill-conditioned hair harshened by chemical rinses and drying permanents. Makes its texture softer, silkier.
3. Persuades hair to dress more easily, wave to remain longer.

TRESSGLO comes in a box containing 3 organdie bags, each one sufficient for one rinse — to be brewed by you or your hairdresser as easily as a cup of tea. $1.00

HOUSE OF HERBS, Inc.
Juniper Hills, Canaan, Conn.

Farm & Garden Shop

39 Newbury Street
Boston

HERB VINEGARS

Culinary-dried herb combinations
Herb Vinegars
Horehound Candy
Herb Plants

SHERMAN K. AND VERA B. HARDY
Eighty Hill Street, Lexington, Mass.

Originators of the Herb-Bar

For sale at
FARM & GARDEN SHOPS
BOSTON AND NEW YORK

READY TO USE
HERB GARDENS

Each Garden complete with
1 — Sturdy, young, culinary herb plants.
2 — Blue-print with six suggested lay-outs.
3 — Letter to the gardener with instructions for planting and care of garden.
4 — Letter to the cook with suggestions for astonishing new dishes and surprises for re-making old ones.

Little Herb Garden No. 1
71 plants—Price complete, $7.50

Little Herb Garden No. 2
91 plants—Price complete, $10.50

Supply limited — Shipping date about May 15th

RANCOCAS HERBS
218 High Street
Mount Holly, N. J.

GARDEN FRESH HERB BLENDS
Saw Mill Farm
NEW CITY, ROCKLAND COUNTY, N.Y.

FOODS FOR THE EPICURE
include

Sorrel Soup
Grape Catsup
Herbed Hickory Salt
Cocktail Artichokes
Tomato and Basil Relish
Purée de Topinambour
Tomato Marmalade with Basil
Pear Chips with Lemon Balm
Wine Vinegar with Herb Bouquet
and
Saw Mill Farm Seasoning Wheels

which are permanent kitchen fixtures, convenient, practical, decorative, available in three sizes and several combinations.

Price List upon Application

"Fare on the Farm," a booklet of suggestions, information and recipes   25 cents

---

AN HERB PRIMER

by G. M. BROWN

TOPSFIELD, MASS.

New and revised edition   *50 cents*

HERBS
FROM
THE LITTLE HOUSE
ANNISQUAM, MASS.

PLANTS · DRIED HERBS

SEND FOR FREE CATALOG

HERB PLANTS

New England Grown for Northern Gardens

100 varieties
and
Sweet-Leaved
Geraniums

Catalogue on request

HIGHMEAD NURSERY, Inc.
Dept. 9
Ipswich, Mass.

HERBS

HERB PLANTS: pot-grown, easily shipped: spring, summer and fall.

DRIED HERBS: home-grown, dated, carefully prepared, single ingredients as well as our own popular blends for Salads, Omelets, Soups, Poultry Stuffing, Tomato Recipes, Sauces, etc.

HERB COOKERY: attractive Booklet, just published, with excellent Recipes for Herbs, sent on receipt of 25 cents.

HERB CATALOGUE: listing over 100 varieties, with cultural direction, etc., sent on receipt of 10 cents.

WEATHERED OAK HERB FARM, Inc.
Bradley Hills, Bethesda, Maryland

CHARLES H. MERRYMAN,
President and General Manager

STONECROP HERB SHOP
WOODSTOCK, NEW YORK

Old-fashioned Herbs and Antiques
Ready to Use Mixtures for Meat-Fish-Salad-
Omelet-Stews. Any three in box postpaid
east of Mississippi, $1.25
Herb Mustards, Vinegars and Salts
Books on Growing and Cooking with Herbs

When you come to

WILLIAMSBURG, VIRGINIA,

as all the world is now doing, you will enjoy visiting

THE HERB & GARDEN SHOP

in its attractive setting which reflects the charm of this Colonial City. Do come in to see us.

THE HERB & GARDEN SHOP
Specialists in Culinary Herbs

on Nicholson Street near
the Colonial Gaol in Williamsburg, Virginia

Visit
CHENEY'S HERB GALLERY

The most complete display of condimental and medicinal herbs in the United States. The display includes all of the dried flowers used in Pot Pourris and Floral Mixtures. Attic-tied herbs both medicinal and condimental are here shown.

Gallery is open from 9.00 a.m. to 5.00 p.m. daily. An attendant can be had by appointment.

G. S. CHENEY CO.
15 UNION STREET, BOSTON

MEDICINAL AND CULINARY HERBS

Lose Their Value with Age

You can get strictly fresh, last season's crop of Herbs, Roots, Berries, Barks, etc.

DIRECT FROM
INDIANA BOTANICAL GARDENS

Headquarters for Medicinal Roots and Herbs for over 30 years

**P. O. Box 5
HAMMOND, INDIANA
Dept. H**

Write for our colored, illustrated *Herbalist Almanac*

The HERBARIST

A Publication of
The Herb Society of America

No. 8

For Use and for Delight

BOSTON, MASSACHUSETTS

1942

Newcomb & Gauss Co., Printers
Salem, Massachusetts

Copyright, 1942, By The Herb Society of America

CONTENTS

	PAGE
FRONTISPIECE: Iris tectorum	4
Original etching by Caroline Weir Ely	
CHALLENGE OF 1941 . . *Commercial Research Committee*	5
CHAMOMILE . . . . *Albert F. Hill*	9
SILPHIUM . . . . . . *Martha Genung Stearns*	17
WATER CLOCKS . . . . *Edith Scott*	23
ELIZABETH BLACKWELL AND HER CURIOUS HERBAL	
Emily Read Cheston	24
OF CONSERVATION INTEREST — THE SASSAFRAS TREE . . .	27
THE GRADATIONS OF THE FLAVOR CHART . . *Vera B. Hardy*	29
THRIFT FOR DEFENSE—	
FORGOTTEN LORE	30
FORGOTTEN HAND-BOOKS . . *Elizabeth R. Van Brunt*	31
FORGOTTEN POT-HERBS . . . . *Frances Williams*	32
FORGOTTEN BEE-PLANTS	33
LEMON VERBENA . . . . . . *Mary E. Fitz-Gerald*	36
OF GARDEN INTEREST	38
FIELD NOTES	40
THE HERB SOCIETY OF AMERICA: Officers and Directors . .	43

IRIS TECTORUM
Original etching by Caroline Weir Ely

THE CHALLENGE OF 1941

THE shortage of the imported herb caused by the war, has affected many industries, not only the medicinal supply houses, the paint industry, the distilleries, the spice trade—the grinders, perfume and cosmetic industry, but a host of smaller groups, requiring particular herb or herbs for the continuance of their industry.

Efforts of the industries themselves, to experiment with the production on American soil, of the particular herbs needed, have been limited; a notable exception are the experiments conducted in Kentucky, on anise, caraway, fennel, angelica, and liquorice, and their relation to the essential oil industry.*

It would have been ideal to co-ordinate these various interests so that a growing program could have been undertaken, in co-operation with the department of agriculture; since statistics showed that the imported herb would be but a minor crop, grown in this country, such a project of necessity gave way to larger interests.

As the story of the scarcity of the different herbs became publicized, there were thousands of inquiries directed to every known source of information, the Herb Society became a clearing house for many of these inquiries, analysis of a thousand of these letters taken at random gives an interesting cross section of the result of such publicity.

Seventy-five percent of these inquiries came from owners of unproductive land, on which it was desired to grow a paying crop, but without experience in growing, or available equipment or labor. *Twenty percent* wished to undertake growing as a defense measure, having gardening experience, but wishing

---

* Lecture to American Society of Agricultural Engineers, Penna. State College, June, 1940. Compilation of research papers, relating to the problems of the cultivation of aromatic plants, for the production of essential oils published by the National Farm Chemurgic Council.

[5]

complete supervision as to what to grow, how to grow, and the disposal of the crop after harvesting. *Five percent* were good growers with equipment except for drying, but reluctant to undertake a crop, for which there was no reliable data as to cultivation, cost or yield in their particular section. Some too having a keen memory of the last war when with the coming of peace, growers were left without a market for an expensively grown crop.

The situation was one of scarcity, scarcity of some medicinal and culinary herbs,—scarcity of knowledge of how to grow commercially in acreage, scarcity of seed or stock from which to grow.

Generalizations and more ink would never make sage or belladonna grow, and so the challenge was met by the Herb Society, by confining its research to a definite program of growing, largely in New England. Keeping records of sage costs, soil and yield, as well as running a fertilizer test of sage, growing test plots of belladonna and digitalis, of which there were already some records.

Digitalis. 5000 plants were distributed to various laboratories and planted under different conditions of soil and location for experiment in potency, and seed selection. The result of this experiment will be spread over a period of five years, since so many factors enter into the potency of the leaf requiring many assays, and assays are costly. It was found in one assay this year that first year digitalis, of luxuriant growth, dried without artificial heat, grown in full sun, in a rich loam was less potent than the wild digitalis grown in Oregon.

Belladonna.* Seven test plots were undertaken in different localities, plants were grown in the greenhouse, and in May transplanted into the field, being then six inches high. Twelve percent of the crop was lost to cut-worms, but with frequent cultivation, and spraying with non-poisonous insecticide, the plants gave a good crop of seed and leaf with good potency.

* Belladonna, by Dr. H. Youngken, *Herbarist*, 1940.

Since the roots are likely to winter-kill in New England, and must be taken up like dahlia bulbs, it would seem that this crop was best adapted to the West Coast, except for a leaf crop. In the last war twenty-four growers successfully cultivated some 96 acres in California.

Sage. The records* of this year's growing form an excellent basis for the growing of next year's crop. The growers have been alert to the needs of machinery adapted to the crop, in order to reduce labor costs. One grower has developed a practical hand-power harvester, another a workable stripper, when the requirements call for leaf sage. It may seem discouraging in reading the records, that so many acres were abandoned on account of poor germination, and the weed problem, during this season of abnormal drought, but the acres which were saved demonstrated that under the most trying conditions, sage can be grown in New England, at a cost not prohibitive to the buyer, in normal times. The yield may be increased to average 1500 pounds of dry sage an acre, with a goal of 2000. If at the coming of peace, buyers continue to buy these products abroad, on account of the price, then the American growers have failed to meet the challenge of holding their own market,—by growing a better crop, though at a slightly higher price, and buyers will lose the assurance of a more stable crop,—a challenge not only to the growers, but to those studying plant genetics and experimenting with chromosomes. Better methods and better stock is the goal of 1942.

* Bulletin 1, Notes on Growing Sage, Jan. 1, 1940.   Bulletin 2, Records of Sage Growing and Fertilizer Tests, Jan., 1942.

Commercial Research Committee.

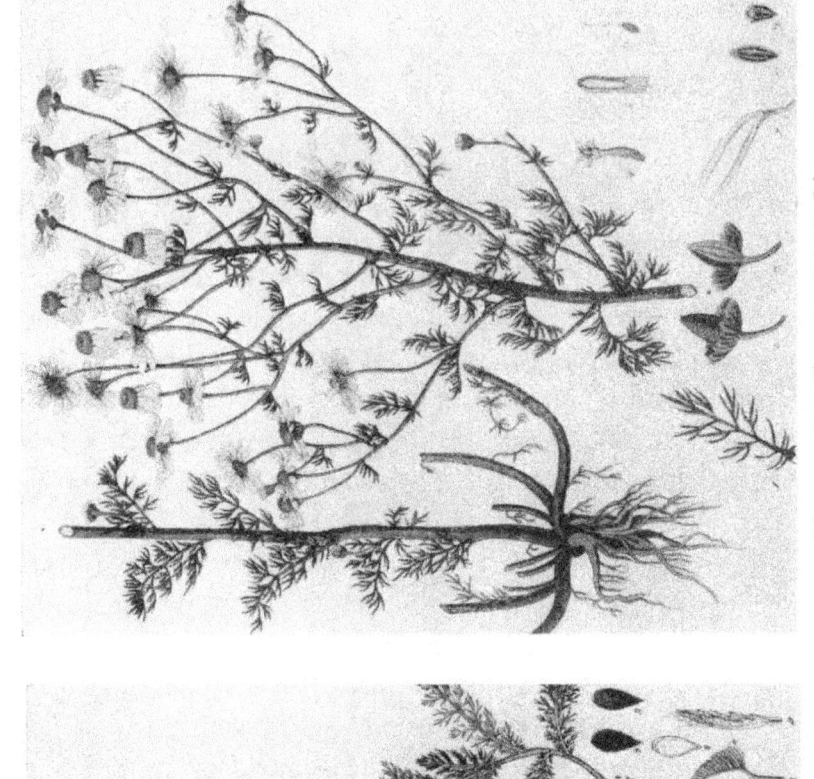

ANTHEMIS NOBILIS *Linnaeus*

Reproduced from Hayne, Arzneigewächse 10 (1827) t. 47. (*Courtesy of the Botanical Museum of Harvard University.*)

MATRICARIA CHAMOMILLA *Linnaeus*

Reproduced from Hayne, Arzneigewächse 1 (1805) t. 3. (*Courtesy of the Botanical Museum of Harvard University.*)

CHAMOMILE
ALBERT F. HILL

CHAMOMILE, or Camomile, is a very old inhabitant of our gardens, long esteemed for virtues both real and imagined. The literature of medical botany, folklore and horticulture, both past and present, is full of references to this herb and its many uses.

It is often difficult, however, to identify with accuracy the particular plant under discussion since the name "chamomile" has been used for a dozen or more species in some six genera. *Anthemis* and *Matricaria* are the principal genera concerned, with such familiar species as *Anthemis arvensis, A. Cotula, A. nobilis, A. tinctoria, Matricaria Chamomilla, M. glabrata, M. inodora* and *M. parthenioides*. Of these only two are of importance, the majority of references to chamomile applying either to *Anthemis nobilis* L. or to *Matricaria Chamomilla* L.

Confusion also exists in regard to these two species. Not only do writers fail to differentiate between them, or erroneously attribute characteristics of one species to the other, but the name "Common Chamomile" may be used for either species depending on the locality. In England, and usually in the United States, chamomile is *Anthemis* and Common Chamomile *A. nobilis;* in Europe chamomile is *Matricaria* and Common Chamomile is *M. Chamomilla*. It is impossible to state which interpretation is correct. In the first edition of Standardized Plant Names "Common Chamomile" was reserved for *Anthemis nobilis,* and *Matricaria Chamomilla* was called "False Chamomile." In the second edition of this work *Matricaria Chamomilla* is designated as "German Chamomile" while *Anthemis nobilis* becomes "Roman Chamomile." All this confusion is regrettable and unnecessary since the plants themselves are perfectly distinct and possess adequate scientific names of long standing.

Anthemis nobilis *Linnæus* Species Plantarum (1753) 984

Anthemis nobilis is a low growing, creeping or trailing perennial herb with a small much branched rhizome and numerous slightly hairy, prostrate, ascending or sometimes erect stems, which are freely branched and often root at the base. The whole plant is downy and pleasantly aromatic. The leaves are alternate, sessile, 1-2 inches long, blunt, very deeply 2-3-pinnate with numerous crowded short linear acute more or less hairy gray-green segments, so threadlike as to give the whole plant a feathery appearance. The few flower heads are solitary and terminal on long erect pubescent peduncles, which are woolly when young. The involucral scales are few in number occurring in 2 or 3 rows. They are adpressed, broadly oblong, blunt, with wide transparent membranous scarious lacerated borders and a slightly wooly mid-rib. The receptacle is solid, very conical, and bears between each floret, minute thin linear blunt often slightly hairy scarious chaffy scales, which are a little shorter than the disk flowers. The disk flowers are small, yellow, perfect, and very numerous, with a tubular corolla which is campanulate above, cylindrical and somewhat dilated at the persistent base, and bears a few oil glands on the outside. The ray flowers are fewer in number (12-20) and pistillate. The limb of the ligulate corolla is oval-oblong, 3-toothed at the apex and white. The branches of the stigma are recurved with brush-like ends. The fruit is a very small dry somewhat 3-angled smooth slightly compressed achene with three faint ridges on the inner face. There is no pappus, but the fruit is crowned by the persistent base of the corolla. The receptacle becomes more conical as the fruit matures. This species flowers in late summer.

Under cultivation, varieties are produced with double flowers in which all or nearly all of the tubular flowers have been converted into white ligulate flowers. These double flowers are larger, whiter and more showy, but cannot be grown from seed.

Anthemis nobilis is a common wild plant of western and

southern Europe, occurring from Portugal and Spain, through western and central France and Italy to Dalmatia and possibly to Germany and southern Russia. It is quite common in England, especially in the south, and extends to Ireland and to the western islands off Scotland. It is also a favorite garden plant. This species is frequently grown in the United States (it might well be called Garden Chamomile) and may occur as an escape from cultivation. This plant has been grown commercially in Belgium, England, France and Germany.

While it is impossible to identify with certainty the chamomile of Dioscorides and other classical and ancient authors, since there are so many plants with similar daisy-like inflorescences, it is possible to eliminate certain species from consideration. *Anthemis nobilis* could not have been known to the peoples of antiquity as it did not occur in the Italy of that period, in Greece or in Asia Minor. It does not seem to have been observed in Europe until after the Middle Ages when, according to Gesner, it was carried from Spain to Germany. That it was not an ancient German plant is borne out by the fact that there are no names for it in Old German. The first references to this species are to be found in the Anglo-Saxon herbals and Middle English medical books where it is known under a number of names, chief of which is *maythen*. This old Saxon name for chamomile continued to be used in England for hundreds of years. We may safely assume that *Anthemis nobilis* was first used and cultivated in England. It must have been grown for centuries prior to the end of the 16th Century for at that time it was a common weed near London, and the double variety was also known. It had also become established on the continent for Camerarius noted its abundance near Rome in 1598 and gave it the name Roman Chamomile.

Anthemis nobilis has enjoyed an amazing reputation as a domestic medicinal plant and was extensively used in early days. There were almost no human ailments which chamomile was not supposed to alleviate or cure, and it was also valued as the "plant's physician," in the belief that its presence in a garden tended to keep all the other plants in a healthy condition. While most of the supposed virtues have proved to be non-existent in the light of modern medical science, Anthemis is still a valuable medicinal plant, particularly in England where it is known as Roman Chamomile. Both the dried flower heads and an essential oil which is distilled from the flowers (or from the whole plant) are utilized.

The Roman chamomile flowers used in medicine are always the double flowers obtained from cultivated plants, although these contain a smaller amount of the medicinal principles. One of the constituents is an aromatic bitter which makes the flowers valuable as a stimulant, carminative and tonic, at least in moderate doses. In large doses they are emetic. They may be used as an antiperiodic or as a useful stomachic in the treatment of dyspepsia and flatulence. For many years they were used for poultices and fomentations.

The oil, which was known as early as 1677, has similar properties. Valuable for its stimulant antispasmodic and carminative action, it is much used as a tonic and bitter stomachic. It is often added to purgative pills to prevent griping. The oil is bright blue in color when first distilled, but becomes yellow or brown on exposure to the air.

The medicinal value of *Anthemis nobilis* is not the only reason why this species has been a favorite garden plant for so many years. The creeping habit of the plant makes it a valuable substitute for grass as a ground cover. On dry banks and in arid places generally it soon forms a flat compact mat. Chamomile lawns have long been a familiar feature of the English landscape, the moist climate keeping the plants bright green, thick and vigorous. Such lawns have not succeeded as well in the drier climate of the United States. In Elizabethan gardens this chamomile was much used on banks and for turf seats, while in modern gardens it is utilized for walks, paths, the interspaces between the knots of formal gardens and similar places. English gardeners are coming to feel that Anthemis tends to exhaust the soil of its nutrient material, a far cry from the old belief that it was the plant's doctor. Fragrant when crushed and uninjured by trampling feet (a characteristic long recognized) or the passing of a lawn mower, this plant should be more widely used. The intriguing name "Whig Plant" was given to this species during the American Revolution because, like the Whigs, it throve better for being trampled on and kept prostrate.

Matricaria Chamomilla *Linnæus* Species Plantarum (1753) 891

Matricaria Chamomilla is an annual herb with an erect solid smooth shining strongly striate pale green stem, one to two feet in height and much branched, with long slender branches. The leaves are numerous, alternate, sessile with a dilated base partly surrounding the stem, oblong-oval, obtuse, 2-3-pinnate with narrow setaceous acute curved spreading smooth bright green segments. The flower heads are numerous, terminating the slender glabrous branches and forming a more or less corymbose inflorescence. They are small, about 5/8 of an inch in diameter. The flat involucre consists of a single row (sometimes 2 or 3 rows) of from 10-30 very small equal linear blunt smooth imbricated scales with scarious brownish ends and transparent margins. The receptacle, at first broadly ovoid and solid, becomes elongated, conical, ovoid and hollow. It is smooth and lacks scales. The disk flowers are perfect, very small and numerous with a pale greenish yellow, deeply 5-toothed tubular corolla which has a few oil glands on the outside. The anthers have a large terminal appendage. The ray flowers are rather numerous (15-25), crowded, overlapping and pistillate. The limb of the corolla is barely ¼ of an inch long, oval-oblong, faintly and bluntly 2-3-lobed at the apex, white, involute and erect in the bud, spreading in the flower and afterwards quickly deflexed. The styles are spreading.

The fruit is a very small oblong-ovoid smooth pale gray achene, somewhat curved, with five faint ribs on the concave side and crowned with a slightly raised border. There is no pappus. This species flowers in July and August. There are no double varieties.

The principal differences between *Matricaria Chamomilla* and *Anthemis nobilis* may be summarized as follows: smaller size, annual rather than perennial habit, coarser leaves, somewhat corymbose rather than solitary flower heads, elongated and hollow rather than conical and solid receptacles, and the absence of scales between the florets.

Matricaria Chamomilla is a Eurasian species found throughout Europe from the Mediterranean region north to England and southern Scandinavia and eastward to the Ural Mountains. In Asia it is native in the Caucasus, Asia Minor, Persia, Afghanistan and northern India. It occurs as a weed in China, Australia and the United States where it is occasional on ballast ground and in other waste places. Because of its habitat it might well be designated Wild Chamomile.

This species was known to the Greeks and Romans and may have been the chamomile to which Dioscorides and other writers of antiquity refer, although this is open to question. It has been used by the German people from earliest time, as is evidenced by the fact that it was once considered sacred to Balder, the Sun God, and by the numerous names for the plant in Old German. *Matricaria Chamomilla* is extensively cultivated in Europe, and has a place in all peasant gardens. It is grown on a commercial scale in Hungary, Belgium, Russia, Poland and Germany. Our word *Chamomile* and the specific epithet *Chamomilla* are derived from the Greek words *chamai* (on the ground) and *melon* (apple). This is most appropriate since the plant is low and pleasantly aromatic throughout with an odor suggestive of ripe apples.

Matricaria Chamomilla finds its chief use in medicine. Always preferred on the continent of Europe, this German or

Hungarian Chamomile, of the drug trade has now almost completely supplanted *Anthemis nobilis* for such purposes in the United States, and is the only chamomile recognized as official in this country at the present time. Its properties are similar to those of Anthemis. A hot infusion of the dried flower heads is used as a carminative, tonic and gastric stimulant. It is particularly valuable in cases involving poor digestion, convalescence or general debility.

One of the most interesting uses of Matricaria is as the source of a herb tea or tisane. The French, who are perhaps the greatest connoisseurs and certainly the greatest users of these aromatic beverages, include chamomile as one of the six most favored herbs. These tisanes play an important part in French daily life, as well as constituting the first cure for ailments not serious enough to require the services of a doctor. The increasing number of devotees of herb teas in this country find themselves agreeing with the French that Matricaria yields a much more pleasant and soothing beverage than does Anthemis, and one highly to be recommended as a nightcap.

In Spain, Matricaria flowers are used to flavor one of the lightest of their sherries, which is known by the Spanish name for chamomile, *Manzanilla*. Experiments are now being carried on with these flowers as a possible flavoring ingredient of domestic Vermouth.

An extract of Matricaria flowers is much used in beauty parlors as a wash for blonde or light red hair. The tonic properties of the chamomile are beneficial and the dark amber liquid seems to bring out the natural color of the hair. The flowers of *Anthemis nobilis* are sometimes utilized for this purpose but the light amber extract obtained from these is not considered as efficacious.

The essential oil extracted from *Matricaria Chamomilla* flowers is reported to be a solvent for platinum chloride and is used in the glass and porcelain industries in the process of coating containers with platinum. This oil also finds a use in the perfume industry as a blend in some of the oriental compounds, often in combination with pachouli, lavender and oak moss.

References to the use of Matricaria as a ground cover are apt to be confusing. It is obvious that this annual species is not suitable for a permanent cover, such as lawns, path, etc. It does, however, form satisfactory mats for sunny, gravelly banks and may even be cut back with a lawn mower, but such use is only temporary.

Research Department of
The Botanical Museum of
Harvard University.

WAR brings strange inventions. It was in one of the Chinese conflicts attendant with famine, that the roof Iris commenced to be grown on the thatched roofs. Owing to the need of land for all foods it was forbidden to plant anything in the ground not for practical purposes. However certain Iris only could supply the powder with which the women whitened their faces, and they would not be cheated of that. "Must we look like frights as well as die of hunger?" they cried, and so every woman set a tiny plantation of Iris on the roof of her house. They are still so grown in the Orient, and in France. Or were! The variety is known by the descriptive name, *Iris tectorum*, grows to a height of 12-16 inches, in two colors, a blue-lavender, and the far more beautiful white, the subject of the etching on page 4.

SILPHIUM, THE WONDER PLANT
MARTHA GENUNG STEARNS

WHEN one observes an ancient silver coin bearing the image of an emperor on one side and an ungainly bulbous plant on the reverse, one naturally asks what plant this can be, whose uses or properties were so important as to make it thus worth its weight in precious metal? It must have played a most significant part in the national fortunes of its country to be so honored.

It was, according to ancient writers, a plant called Silphium or Laserpitium, of the family of umbelliferæ, common to Syria, Media and Libya, and called in Greek Thapsia Silphion, which was exported from Cyrene to Greece in great quantities in ancient times and was sold by weight at the same rate as silver. It is to the Cyrenaican silver coinage of about 500 B.C. and to a description by Theophrastus that we owe our knowledge of it. Its family history and relationships lead into all sorts of conjecture and romance, but enough remains to prove its honorable service to the realm of Cyrene where it played an important part in commerce.

Down through the centuries and in all the old countries, there have been special plants which have had a reputation as a cure-all or drug with almost magic properties, like ginseng in China and sassafras among the Spanish explorers, and silphium seems to have been one of these throughout the Near East. It was extremely versatile, highly prized as a vegetable, condiment and gum-resin, and designated by the Greeks as a wonder-remedy. It grew wild on the hills and cattle who fed on the thick stalks grew fat, after the first purgative effects wore off, and the flavor of their flesh was said to be greatly improved. In fact, it was its use as cattle-fodder which was responsible for its final disappearance, for Pliny in the first century A.D. says

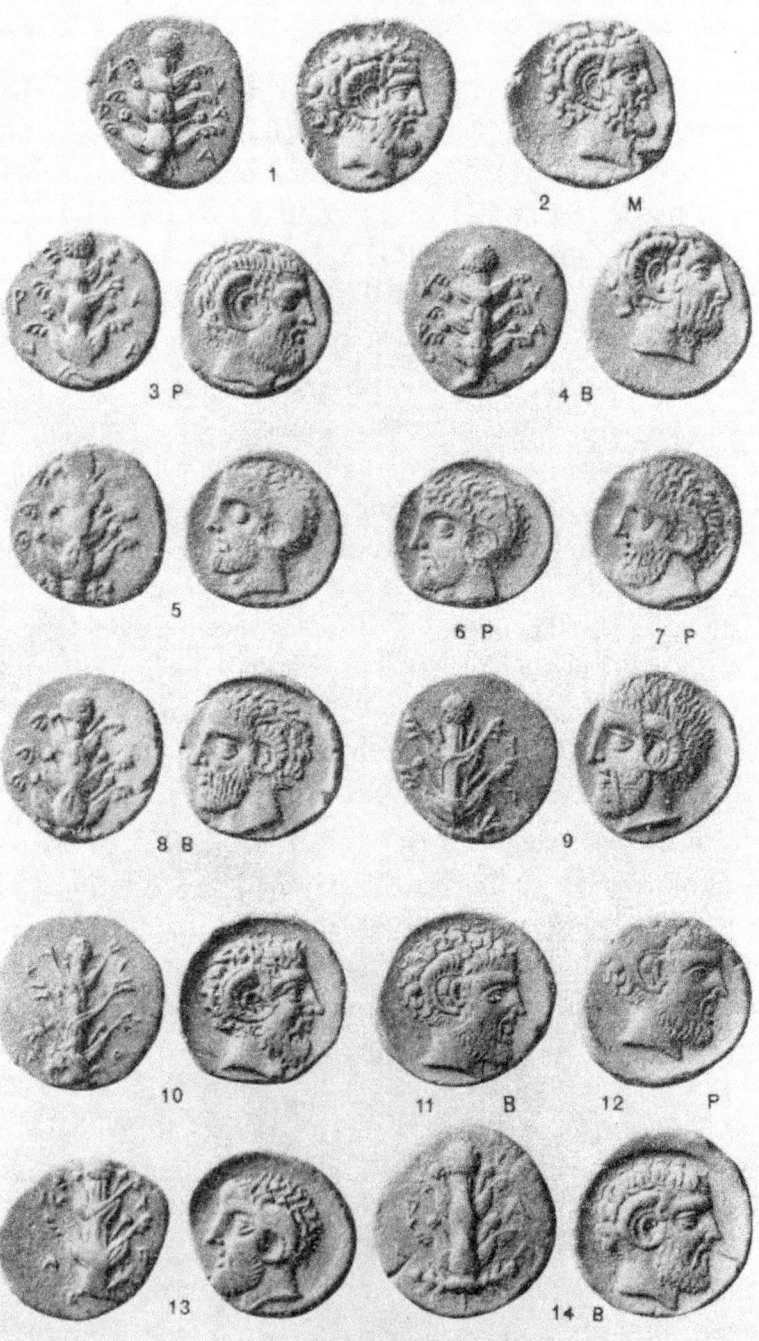

CYRENAICA. PL. VIII.

CYRENE LATE 5th—EARLY 4th CENT.

that "the publicans who rent the pastures dug it up for food for cattle." In the time of Tiberius, a physician prescribed "laser of Cyrenaica, if it can be met with," showing its growing scarcity.

The plant known as Silphium Cyrenaicum received the Latin name of Laser because of its resinous juice. Both the names laser and silphium were applied erroneously to a Persian plant introduced by Alexander the Great; this is ferula assafœtida; from which the drug asafœtida is obtained. Our plant, also known as Thapsia, is something quite different, although it belongs to the same botanical family. Pliny and Linnæus are both responsible for a great confusion of names. In the first place Pliny, in spite of his deep erudition, was rather given to romancing, and some of the particulars he gives with gusto about the origin and properties of the plant sound like folk lore; he also seems to have taken the description of a different plant from older writers and applied it to Laserpitium. Later Linnæus, who started our modern botanical nomenclature, sometimes used classical names for plants other than their originals, and the plant now botanically known in this country as silphium, native to the Mississippi Valley, is not the classical silphium of which we write.

To disentangle the authentic facts about Silphium Cyrenaica is like unravelling a net which spreads widely into history and fable, even carrying us back to the gifts of incense brought to Bethlehem by the Kings from the east. The recognition of its economic importance upon the coinage is reinforced by another portrayal upon a Laconian cup, probably made by Cyrenaic potters about the middle of the 6th century, B.C. It shows the seated figure of King Arcesilas of Cyrene supervising the weighing of silphium; before him men are loading bundles of the drug or gum on to large scales, and below are nets full of similar bundles. Valuable drug plants have been carried by ship and caravan over the trade routes of the world since the earliest times, and in the case of this plant with its manifold uses, the King himself evidently took a hand in its despatch.

Pliny writes at some length of silphium in Chapter 15 of his Natural History and says that the variety growing in Cyrenaica was greatly superior to that of Armenia, Syria or Libya, and that "the Dictator Cæsar, at the beginning of the Civil War, took from out of the public treasury, besides gold and silver, no less than 1500 pounds of laserpitium." The "Rudens" of the playwright Plautus, the scene of which is laid near Cyrene, makes frequent mention of the growth of laserpitium there and the exporting of its resinous gum for use in perfumes and incense. How different is the drama being played now in that ancient city! Only the other day we read in a war correspondent's dispatch: "Cyrene was like a dream to us after our long wanderings in Libya's wastelands. It is a beautiful town, built on the site of an ancient Roman town on wild precipitous hills above the sea . . ."

Let us look at the plant itself. The picture on the coins bears some resemblance to a giant fennel with a thick stalk sheathed by the unopened leaves, with feathery cut foliage and large flower-heads something like those of an onion. The stalk was considered a great vegetable delicacy. The "rhizias" or root-juice, and the "caulias" or stalk-juice which was inferior to it were used as a purgative by the ancient Greeks and Romans; some writers speak of its use in nervous disorders. Apparently these juices would flow easily from an incision, and when allowed to dry formed an aromatic gum.

Pliny says that "within the memory of the present generation" a single stalk of silphium was all that could be found in Cyrenaica and it was sent as a curiosity to the Emperor Nero. That a plant which once played so great a rôle in domestic and civil life should be allowed to dwindle and disappear within the space of a century or so, is a botanical as well as an economic mystery. There are several plants still growing in Greece and the Mediterranean region with some related qualities, but the one-time wonder plant which grew on the hills of Libya and Cyrene and was stored in the national treasury has completely disappeared except for its portrait in silver.

Note on American Silphium. Owing to the confusion of names mentioned above, modern silphium is identified with a genus of composite plants native to North America, chiefly in the Mississippi Valley. Among these is the S. terebinthinaceum or prairie burdock indigenous to Ohio and Michigan which yields a fragrant turpentine-like gum with stimulant and antispasmodic properties. S. perfoliatum is also called the turpentine sunflower. Still another is the S. laciniatum or compass plant, also called polar plant, whose interesting habit is to grow sideways so that the edges of the flower leaves point north and south; this grows on the prairies of Michigan and Wisconsin and westward. Under "Laserpitium" in the medical dictionaries, we find L. latifolium, white gentian, with a bitter tonic root. Eleven varieties of the genus are considered distinct in the United States, most of them evidently with the characteristic action of root or juice, and producing an aromatic gum; it is a strongly marked and most interesting family.

Mrs. Foster Stearns
Washington
D. C.

IT doth not require a great deal of the Spirit of Prophecy to say that as long as the world lasts, the Pleasures and Entertainments which Gardening and Agriculture afford, will be the pursuit of wise men.

John Lawrence. *A New System of Agriculture.* 1726

Chinese Water Clock

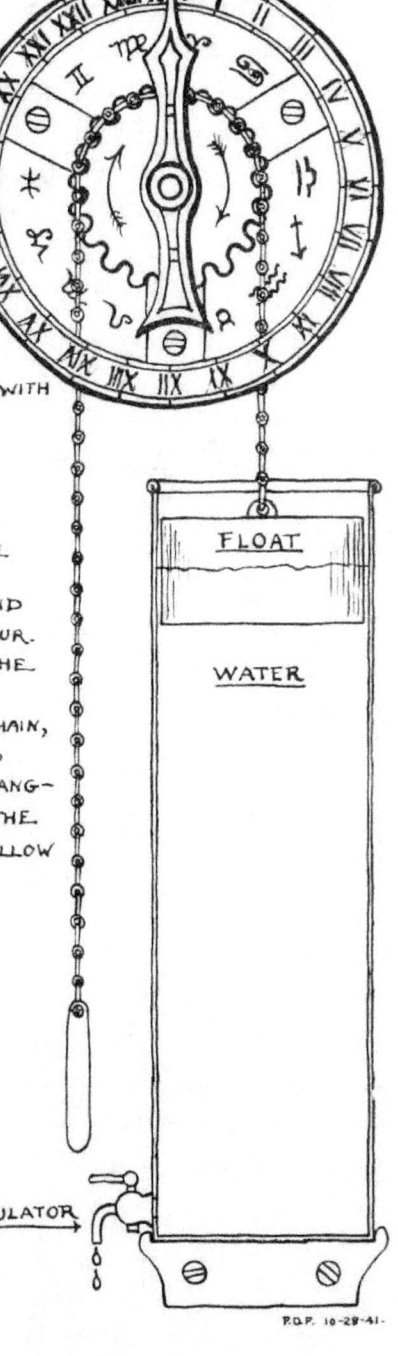

One of the oldest and simplest forms of mechanical clocks known. It consists of a Cylindrical Tank, a Float, a Spigot, a piece of Ladder Chain, a Dial, a Sprocket, and one Hand.

To start the clock, the tank is filled with water. This raises the float to the top. As the water leaks out of the spigot one drop at a time, the float falls and turns the sprocket thru the medium of the chain. The hand, being fastened to the sprocket, is set at the correct time by raising the chain from the sprocket and then turning the hand to the proper hour.

By regulating the drip at the spigot, the clock can be made to go fast or slow.

The counterweight on the free end of chain, is to take up the slack. The combined weight of the counterweight and overhanging chain is less than the weight of the float, otherwise the float would not follow the receding water.

WATER CLOCKS
EDITH SCOTT

THE oldest system of measuring time was by the regulated dripping of water. China has records of such a contrivance used over 4000 years ago, and the Greeks called their mechanisms of the type Clepsydra, or Thief of Water. The Clepsydra antedated the sundial by centuries. Dials were primarily for astronomical use and not until 728 B. C. was the augur of the gnomon perfected. Another advantage of water over sun, it tells time at night. Pliny the younger used sludge in his timepiece to have it drip more slowly, in order that he might talk longer! I own two from England, dated 1625 and 1654, made of brass mounted on bog oak. The mechanism is simple; a tube or container with a float of cork or metal attached to a chain passing over a sprocket wheel. As the water drips, the float goes down, and the hand revolves according to the speed of the drip. The speed varies with the size of the clock. My garden clock (illustrated on page 22) has the signs of the zodiac and the numerals for 24 hours. It keeps good time with 27 drops a minute.

Mrs. Arthur Scott
Pennsylvania.

BIBLIOGRAPHY
"The Technical Arts and Sciences of the Ancients," Albert Neuburger, trans. by Henry S. Brose. Macmillan.
"Old Clocks and Watches," F. J. Britten, chap. 1, pp. 9-14.
Bulletin of the Russell-Cotes Art Gallery and Museum, vol. xi, Dec., 1932. Bournemouth.
"Horologes egyptiennes," J. Capart, Bulletin S-3, vol. 10, pp. 50-4, May, 1938.
"Clepsydras," R. W. Sholey, Egyptian Archeological Journal, Nov., 1931, vol. 17, pp. 174-8.
"Timekeeping in Greece and Rome," F. A. Seely, General Appendix to Board of Regents Report, Smithsonian Institution.
The Connoisseur, vol. xxxv, Jan.-Apr., 1913.

ELIZABETH BLACKWELL AND HER "CURIOUS HERBAL"

EMILY READ CHESTON

"IT is a singular fact that physic is indepted for the most complete set of figures of the medicinal plants to the genius and industry of a lady, exerted on an occasion that redounded highly to her praise." So, in 1790, wrote Richard Pulteney in his "Progress of Botany."

The story of Elizabeth Blackwell's life is as "curious" as her herbal to which Pulteney refers. She was the gallant, hard-working and evidently adoring wife of an attractive rascal, Alexander Blackwell, a self-styled "Dr." who had settled himself and his wife in London. Here, when he was unsuccessful in the practice of medicine he undertook to enter the printing business. He belonged to no guild and had never been apprenticed: laws were strict: he was arrested and fined. Having no means whatever of paying the fine he soon found himself in the Debtor's prison.

Elizabeth, who by this time had a child to care for, rose to the occasion. Her education had included drawing and painting and she was in touch with Isaac Rand, a lecturer and demonstrator at the famous "Apothecaries Garden." From all over the world, seeds, roots and plants were being sent to this garden where, under supervision of the great Philip Miller, they were grown and the results reported to the "Company of Apothecaries." So many new plants were being introduced, that there was need for a new illustrated herbal. Upon the advice of Rand, Elizabeth moved into lodgings near the garden and set herself to work.

She was given free access to the garden and drew from life some 500 plants. As the drawings were made she carried them to her husband in prison; there he wrote the descriptions, abridging them from a recognized authority, and supplied the correct names in seven foreign languages (Latin, Greek, Italian, Spanish, Dutch and German). When this was done the indefatigable lady made copper plates not only of the drawings but of the text and finally colored each flower-plate by hand.

The work is accurate and the drawings have the charm and individuality which is only attained when an understanding artist draws from a living specimen. The small explanatory diagrams of seeds, flowers, etc., which accompany some of the plates, are clear and the proportion of each subject to its space is admirable; the coloring has been faithfully done. Under each of the 500 plates appears:—"Eliz. Blackwell delin. Sculp. et Pinx."

In common with all early herbals the descriptions show how very little information was available to the botanists or the doctors of that day. Her work was much admired by Sir Hans Sloane, Philip Miller and the various doctors and botanists connected with the Garden. She made a real position for herself and, to quote Pulteney once more:—"During her abode in Chelsea she was frequently visited by persons of quality and many Scientific people who admired her performance and patronized her undertaking."

When her first volume was finished she was allowed to exhibit her manuscript in person to the College of Physicians and received from that august body not only a present but a testimonial of approval. Being an alert business woman she lost no time in copper-plating and adding to her book this "Publick Recommendation" which reads in part:—"We, whose names are underwritten, having a considerable Number of the Drawings from which the plates are to be engraved and likewise some of the Colour'd Plates, think it a Justice done the Publick to declare our satisfaction with them and our good opinion of the capacity of the Undertaker." Ten eminent names, six of them being those of doctors, are appended. The first volume was published in 1737, the second in 1739.

There is no question that the work was excellently done and that there was a demand for such a book. In 1750, a second edition with additional plates was brought out in Nuremberg by a Dr. Trew who added to the text and translated it into German and Latin.

Little is known of Elizabeth after the "Curious Herbal" was completed. She was not with her husband in Sweden where he had been placed in charge of the royal model farm and five years later executed for treason, although she was, by some accounts, planning to join him there. After his death nothing is known of her or of their child.

The full title of the work, on which her fame rests, reads:— "A curious Herbal containing 500 Cuts of the most useful plants which are now used in the Practise of Physic, engraved on folio copper-plates after drawings taken from life. By Elizabeth Blackwell. To which is added a short description of the plants and their common uses in Physic. 1739."

Mrs. Edward M. Cheston
Ambler, Penn.

LET the housewife be skilful in natural phisic for the benefit of her owne folke and others: for to have a phisition alwaies when there is not very urgent occasion and great necessitie, is not for the profite of the house.

The Countrie Farme. 1600

OF CONSERVATION INTEREST

THE SASSAFRAS TREE

A RECENT survey of the ravages of drought over a wide area of the United States brings to light the fact that the sassafras tree known in America since the early days of the Spanish explorers, is fast disappearing. Its many uses taught to the Spaniards by the Indians have continued popular to the present time.

The commercial value of the sassafras tree is as a source of oil. Some fifty years ago the natural sassafras oil industry was supplanted by artificial sassafras oil made from Japanese camphor oil. Originally the Japanese exported the camphor oil to this country, and the United States made the artificial sassafras oil; in later years Japan cut off exporting this camphor oil, and sought a monopoly in making the artificial sassafras oil.

According to the Department of Commerce, statistics show that between the years 1936-1939 camphor oil imports dropped 818,515 pounds and artificial sassafras oil increased 472,777 pounds.

The war with Japan will eliminate imports of both camphor oil and synthetic sassafras oil, a condition which turns the American consumer back to the natural sassafras oil industry.

A too drastic cutting added to the drought is responsible for the decrease of the sassafras tree; so valuable a tree should not be allowed to die out, and reforestation should be undertaken before it is too late.

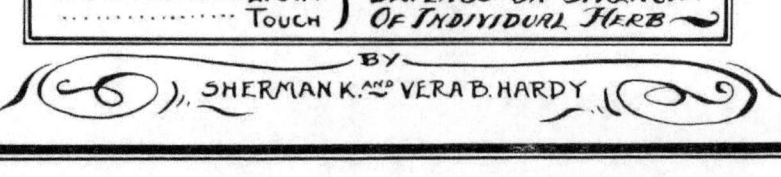

THE GRADATIONS OF THE FLAVOR CHART

THE chart explains two things. First, the different Herbs that may be used to obtain a desirable blend, secondly, the gradations of the flavor and pungency tones of the individual herbs used in these blends. Perfection in the culinary use of herbs is obtained through the use of blends, which consist in properly evaluating the pungency in flavor tones in their relationship to one another.

True blending consists of a build-up of tones wherein no individual herb so predominates as to mask completely the tones of the others. Such combining avoids the repeated use of one herb alone, which is tiring. Since flavor and pungency degree of the individual herb is subject to variations of soil, climate, drying methods and age, the actual quantity of the herb used will vary to meet these changes, and some experimentation may be necessary to meet personal preferences.

The chart is based on the value of the blend after it has been subjected to heat or infusion, but the proportions and amounts of the various ingredients in their fresh state would be approximate. Take the fish blend as example, the basic blend proportion would change little. *Light tones* of Sage, Dill, Tarragon, Lovage, or Parsley. *Strong tones* of Summer Savory, Thyme, or Fennel. *Heavy tone* of Basil. The proper proportions of each determines the successful blend.

WE cannot make so much as a little good pottage without Herbes, which give an admirable relish and make them wholesome for our Bodies.

W. Coles. *The Art of Simpling.* 1656

THRIFT FOR DEFENSE
FROM FORGOTTEN LORE

KNOWLEDGE is an accumulation or merely a succession of acquired facts—the new superimposed upon the old. We must be ever watchful that current enthusiasms do not drive from the memory plant knowledge of other days.

In this war year of 1942, it has seemed wise to recall to mind forgotten possibilities, as true thrift consists in using what is at hand. The home of fifty years ago was not dependent upon the pharmacy; there were sage leaves or gold-thread for canker spot; ragweed seeds for mosquito bites; pennyroyal tea for a cold; hot peppermint tea for a stomach ache; boneset tea for spring inertia; while boiled witch hazen green shoots and leaves eased growing pains.

FETTER LANE SAUSAGE

Fetter Lane wasn't much of a street in Old London, but it held an Inn which drew the crowds. It was merely a little public-house where the kitchen was the only room for entertainment, paved with red bricks, furnished with a few Windsor chairs, and adorned with shining plates of pewter and copper saucepans, scoured until they dazzled the eyes of the guests. Not for these attractions did the diners come, but for the famous sausages of distinctive flavor which bore the name of *Fetter Lane Sausage*. Certain pot-herbs made the difference, and the rule has come down through the decades. Take a pound of pork, fat and lean together; grind it very fine, season with salt and pepper to taste; a full teaspoonful of Sweet Basil with a saltspoonful each of Marjoram and Tarragon; mix all well together and shape into cakes.

THE COLD PACK METHOD IS NOTHING NEW

Twenty-five years ago, more or less, the cold-pack method of preserving food came into prominence, extolled as a new and superior process. In 1812 M. Appert, writing at the order of the French Minister of the Interior, published the book *The Art of Preserving All Kinds of Animal and Vegetable Substances for Several Years*. It was translated into English and ran through several editions, and told of the exact process, illustrated, which swept this country one hundred and five years later. No growing thing is omitted, and in addition Milk and Cream are preserved in the same manner. "Plantes Potagères et Médicinales" (Herbs and Medicinal Plants) occupy the attention of M. Appert, and under the heading "the Juices of Herbs" he says: "I have succeeded in preserving very well the juices of such plants as lettuce, chervil, borage (bourache), wild succory (chicorée sauvage), water-cresses (cresson de fontaine), etc. I prepared them and purified them by the usual process; I corked them, etc., in order to give them one boiling in the water-bath." His "purifying" was our blanching.

FORGOTTEN PRACTICAL HANDBOOKS

Civilian Defense hardens in us a determination to make our families self-supporting—to grow our own and make our own, at least to the extent that may release supplies for the Services and congested areas. To do this, we turn for guidance to the practical handbooks of an earlier generation, culling from the pages what suits our needs.

Three volumes have much that is pertinent. *Art revealed and Universal Guide for the Use of Families,* published in New York in 1854, is a compilation of Herb usages mainly. A plea is made for wider use of native plants, as at that time North America, for its botanical and remedial agents, was perhaps not exceeded by any other land.

Published in 1857 is the *Kitchen Gardener's Instructor* by Thomas Bridgeman, seedsman and florist. Information is clear and terse; 23 aromatic herbs to grow and use; 32 to be cultivated for medicinal and other purposes. Ideal for the practical herb garden of fifty varieties.

The Useful Companion of 1879 compiled by Henry B. Allen

is a volume of vast information of the type to take very seriously.

It is important for each of us in our homes to be more self-reliant, more self-sufficient than this generation has trained us to be. We can well use more planning and forethought as well as artistry in our cooking, and above all else a practice of thrift, a word whose meaning we have lost in the superabundance of our extravagant daily living. More power to the Household Companions!

Elizabeth Remson Van Brunt.
New York

FORGOTTEN POT-HERBS

There are many wild plants and weeds which may be used as food; some have been neglected, while others are still offered for sale in the market.

Sium sisarum, Skirret. Tuberous roots, sugary, on the order of parsnips.

Atriplex hortensis, Orach. Until introduction of spinach this was the favorite pot-herb. Decorative for color in the autumn garden.

Portulaca oleracea, var. sativa, Purslane.* Cook it till tender and heat in butter. Sometimes seen in the market. None should be allowed to go to waste.

Rumex acetosa and *Rumex scutatus,* Garden Sorrel and French Sorrel. Both are good, the last not so bitter. For soup, salad or greens.

Stellaria media, Chickweed. A pleasant addition to salads.

Campanula Rapunculus, Rampion. Roots are radish-like.
(Nicholas County, West Virginia, has a festival in honor of the "rampion" which grows wild in the region, but the plant so-called is the Wild Leek, or Allium tricoccum).

Lepidum sativum. Garden Cress. Good in salads. In Toronto it is forced in the spring and sold when two inches high—little plants in baskets—to be used in cream cheese for sandwiches.

[32]

Chenopodium album, Lamb's-quarters. Greens, offered for sale by the bushel in the Reading Terminal Market in Philadelphia.

Phytolacca decandra, Pokeweed. Forced in the greenhouse like early rhubarb, sold by the bunch, it has pinkish tips and pale yellowish stems. Cooked with pork. For sale in Knoxville, Tennessee, and Philadelphia.

REFERENCES

Herbs by Mrs. Hollis Webster.
Edible Wild Plants by Medsger. Seventy-five salad and pot-herbs listed in Northeastern America for eating.
Types of Greens and Pot-herbs used in Rural Utah Homes, Circular No. 104 of the Utah Agricultural Station, Logan, Utah. Lists twenty cultivated greens and seventeen wild greens.

Mrs. Frances Williams,

Winchester, Mass.

* Cooking rules for Purslane, Skirret and other pot-herbs are given in "Garden of Herbs" by Eleanor S. Rohde.

FORGOTTEN BEE PLANTS

Dr. Robert Cushman Murphy, expert on Conservation, reports that through the wide and indiscriminate use of poison sprays over large areas, the numbers of bees are lessening in an alarming degree. Bees mean fertilization. The individual gardener can do little, perhaps, but every plant saved that attracts the bees is a help.

AN HERB

One which has been neglected, lost, refound and welcomed, is the fragrant Giant Anise-Hyssop, *Agastache anethiodora,* at one time a widely distributed native from Lake Superior and Manitoba to Nebraska westward. The Indians used it for a beverage, seasoning, remedial purposes, and with their tribes it disappeared, although as late as 1872, H. A. Terry, pioneer nurseryman of Council Bluffs, Iowa, harvested a fine crop of honey from his bees that gleaned from the anise-Hyssop. In 1937 Frank C. Pellett, editor of the American Bee Journal, succeeded in obtaining plants from 180 miles north of Winni-

ANISE-HYSSOP — *Agastache anethiodora*

peg, and from this beginning has been built up an abundant supply of the flowers over which the bees work during a period of about five months.

This plant is also to be found along the border sections of S. W. Texas into Mexico and known by the native Mexicans as the "Candy Plant"—No cactus candy made by the Mexicans is complete without the flavoring of Agastache.

Other bee plants are *Cleome lutea*, yellow Spider Flower; *Cassia Marilandica*, Wild Senna; Liatris; Lespedeza; and *Actinomeris alternifolia*, Wingstem.

IT is not only the humanising influence of the garden, it is the democratising influence too. You can get on terms with anybody if you will discuss gardens.

Alpha of the Plough. *Essays*

This picture is taken from a book of Latin poems by Cardinal Francis Barberini, afterward Pope Urban VIII, printed in 1631. The three bees which figure on the coat of arms of this illustrious Roman family are shown here at work drawing sweetness from the soil, in a device taken "from an ancient gem. Three [Bees] mark three things of special power: The Supreme Power, the sown fields of cultivated land, the making of honey."

LEMON VERBENA

LIPPIA CITRIODORA, Lemon Verbena is a native of Chile and Peru, grown in warm climates in the open, and indoors farther north, mainly for its delightful lemon fragrance. The three whorled leaves are narrow and rough, with the mid-summer flowers white or pale colored, borne in pyramidal panicles. Lippia was named for Francois Joseph Lipp, naturalist of Vienna, and contemporary of Linneus, and botanically the species resembles Lantana, another member of the Verbenaceae, rather than Verbena itself. Confusion comes from the plant's appearance under the scientific names of *Aloysia citriodoro; Verbena triphylla; Lippia triphylla; Lippia citriodora*, and a common title *Yerba Louisa*, of Mexican tradition. When Emperor Maximilian and Empress Carlotta began their tragic adventure in Mexico in 1864, they enlarged the splendid urban gardens of the Montezuma palace. It was not considered kingly to cultivate plants for utility or profit, so the gardens were made to abound in fragrant herbs. Among others was the delicious lemony plant, and these imperial exiles named it Yerba Louisa after Carlotta's mother, wife of the Belgian king Leopold.

The term Verbena Oil is often heard, with the conclusion that Lippia citriodora is used in its manufacture, but the U. S. Department of Agriculture has this to say:

> "Inasmuch as its price is out of proportion to its value, the oil is not an article of commerce. For most purposes, it can be replaced by the much cheaper Lemon Grass Oil, which for this very reason is known as East Indian Verbena Oil. Inasmuch as genuine Verbena Oil is but rarely to be had, statements concerning it must be taken with some reserve."

Although seeds were imported from Europe before the war started, propagation of the Lemon Verbena is mostly done by taking cuttings of new growth. Early in the Fall bring in the plants and for a while give very little water while they go through a rest period. In February shake off the dust and trim the weaker growth, pot in fresh soil and place in the sunlight, watering freely. New growth springs up in the course of a few weeks and these new shoots can be used nicely for slips.

If possible it is good practise to keep the old plants growing from year to year, as each season adds to the strength of fragrance as with Rosemary. In Tennessee the plants are left in the ground with success, further north, they may survive in the cold frame if cut to the ground. The safest way is to house them during the winter. Increased growing of Lemon Verbena, Lippia citriodora, will assure householders of the pungent, clean scent so desirable in the linen closet and pot-pourri.

Experiments in the cultivation of Lemon Grass in this country have been undertaken by Dr. A. A. Bourne, Chief of Agricultural Research of the United States Sugar Corporation. In 1937-38 some 240 acres were planted on sandy soil not suited for sugar cane. The crop was processed for oil, and studies made as to the usage of the spent grass. This was found to be suitable feed for beef cattle when supplemented with small quantities of protein. Due to the utilization of this by-product, foreign competition (327,661 pounds of Lemon Grass oil from British India imported in 1938) can be fairly met.

Mary Elizabeth Fitz-Gerald
St. Louis, Mo.

PEACE with the earth is the first peace. Unto so great a mystery, no one path leads, but many. They begin in gardens, leading beside the other great mystery of nature, the mystery of the growing green thing.

Henry Beston. *Herbs and the Earth*

OF GARDEN INTEREST

Consider the Soil

Soil requisites for successful herb growing are mainly basic conditions, varied in slight degree for certain types. Good garden soil expressed in terms of deep workable sandy loam so that the roots can go down to find moisture is the general growing medium adapted to herbal needs. Good drainage and sun come first, other adaptations work themselves out. More sand for Marjoram, rich loam for Tarragon and Basil, dry surfaces —rocky—for Thymes, moderate shade and moisture to suit the Mints. *Any manure mulch in the early fall increases growth which will not endure the winter.* Herbs need no coddling, they ask merely for sun, deep soft root runs, a neutral soil (if acid apply lime) and humus for food, not protection.

Non-Poisonous Insecticides

There is little excuse for using poisonous sprays and dusts in the home area, even for the ornamental plants, and with the vegetables and herbs it is not allowable. Bulletins of the U. S Department of Agriculture, and State Departments of Chemistry and Agriculture restrict the use of arsenicals and fluorides on fruits and vegetables. In spite of these warnings, it has been necessary to condemn and destroy hundreds of car-loads of food stuffs. In the search for substitutes for arsenical and fluorine materials, attention centers in the age old febrifuge, Pyrethrum, the Feverfew of gardens. Rotenone from the roots of Cubé, a plant growing in abundance in the tropics also offers effective relief as a non-poisonous insecticide. It is 30 times as toxic as lead arsenate as a stomach poison, and 15 times as toxic as nicotine as a contact insecticide. Its limiting factor is the rapid deterioration of its toxic qualities. Continued experimentation indicates that by certain processes liquid extracts of rotenone and pyrethrum can be stabilized for an indefinite period of time, and that the toxic qualities of dusts for a period six to ten times greater than dusts non-processed. A concentrated pyrethrum dust has been perfected, one pound of which mixed with talc, sulphur or other cheap inert diluents locally available, will make ten pounds of completed insecticide dust, which retains its pyrethrin strength over a long period. In choosing any liquid or dry insecticide for the herbs, ascertain that it is one of the non-poisonous types.* Any pyrethrum product is extremely toxic to insects and harmless to man and warm-blooded animals.

Labeling the Herb Garden

In the oldest botanical garden of France, the *Ecole des Plantes* of Montpellier, plants are designated by colored labels, selected for the use of the plant, and not its variety. In private gardens such a custom removes the possibility of using wormwood in the salad—or picking belladonna seeds for plums.

Red—Medicinal   Yellow—Culinary
Blue—Industrial   Green—Forage
Black—Poisonous   Purple—Aromatic
     Striped—Suspicious—use not determined

* U. S. Dept. of Agriculture Bulletin E-343.
* The Development of Safer Insecticides for the Home Gardener, C. B. Gnadinger, McLaughlin Gormley King Co., Minneapolis, Minn.

TALK of perfect happiness or pleasure, and what place was so fit for that, as the garden place, wherein Adam was set to be the Herbarist.

John Gerard. The Herball. 1597

FIELD NOTES

OF CHEMURGIC INTEREST

Chemurgy—that new word—a short way of saying—"New crops in place of surplus crops; industrial uses for old and new crops—farm waste turned to profit—".

The minor crops like herbs have a very real place in this program. In proportion as we are increasing the usefulness of these crops, are we helping solve our agricultural problem.

DRUG FROM SWEET CLOVER

Announcement of the proceedings of the Mayo Clinic, Rochester, Minnesota, mentions the discovery of a new chemical in sweet clover, Melilotus alba, which delays the clotting of blood. A cattle disease which was traced to the eating of spoiled sweet clover led to the discovery, and the Wisconsin Agricultural Experiment Station has completed a seven-year study of the new clover-chemical. In the treatment of the formation of blood-clots lodging in the heart or lungs, and in thrombosis, the only practical remedy up to now has been heparin, a liver extract, whose drawback is that it often makes patients ill. Sweet clover seems to have no such ill effects, and the Mayo report states that it may replace heparin in general use. The advantages of this drug are its effectiveness, its prolonged action, and its cheapness.

PAPER FROM SWEET CLOVER STALK

On account of length and strength of the fibres in Sweet Clover, experiments are being made with the fibrous bark of Melilotus toward paper production, not that it could compete with wood in making paper, but it could compare with rags in "rag content," bonds, etc.

A NEW MECHANICAL HARVESTER

A machine which picks clover tops as fast as 2400 hand pickers has been invented by Professor E. N. Gathercoal and Professor P. D. Carpenter of the University of Illinois College of Pharmacy (Urbana, Ill.), who believe it will lead to the development of special apparatus for harvesting more than 200 other medicinal plants. The machine gathered 4 tons of blossoms in a day, while 9 hand pickers got only 6 pounds. No damage is done for subsequent cutting as hay.

THE STAR OF BETHLEHEM

The Star of Bethlehem, Ornithogalum umbellatum, is for gardeners in the main, merely a pretty white flower, in Mediterrean countries it is a source of food. This plant covers the plains of Palestine with its white blooms, and the edible bulbs cooked like chestnuts were formerly stored at Damascus for the use of travelers. It is in recognition of such food usage that the curious Bible reference is made: "And there was a great famine in Samaria, until the fourth part of a cab of *dove's dung* was sold for five pieces of silver" 2 Kings, 6-25. These were the bulbs of the plant which were so nearly gone that the usual store of roots and tubers to be ground into meal became exhausted as the result of the siege, and the price of over three dollars was demanded for the quarter of a cab, or a few ounces.

ANCIENT CHINESE HERBAL

The Library of Congress in Washington which already possesses a notable collection of Chinese Herbals, has recently acquired a splendid example of a much older herbal, printed in P'ing-yang, Shansi, in the year 1249 A. D. Though the set of volumes is not complete, the new acquisition is in excellent condition, printed on paper made of unbleached cotton, with many very clear illustrations. Not only is this herbal an extraordinary piece of book making, but its special interest for herbalists is that it gathers up very early works by generations of Chinese physicians, botanists and scholars into a great compendium of *materia medica,* going back to a work compiled about 1086-1094 by a physician named T'ang Shen-wei on the basis of still earlier herbals. Among the many fine woodcuts are two pictures of the banana plant which must be the oldest extant, and a picture showing two varieties of ephedra, source of the alkaloid ephedrine.

NEW DRUG PLANT

Three years ago a drug plant was brought out of a remote part of China by a National Geographic Society expedition, and was found to be unknown to botanical science. It has now been identified and classified, and Dr. Walter T. Swingle, botanist of the Department of Agriculture, announces its name as *Momordica Grosvenori* in honor of Dr. Gilbert Grosvenor, President of the National Geographic Society. Although its fruit in dried form has long been used by the Chinese as a household remedy for colds, sore throat and minor stomach and intestinal ailments, its genus has hitherto remained a mystery. The Momordica group belongs to the large family of Cucurbitaceæ, the Gourds, and two familiar members of the tribe are M. balsamina, Balsam Apple, and M. charantis, Balsam Pear, annuals used for ornament and screens. The majority of plants with a balsam designation are medicinal. *Echinocystis lobata* is the Wild Balsam Apple, often called the Wild Cucumber.

NATURE'S Time clock. When Lilac buds open, plant the hardy, early things. Plant corn and all moderately tender things when the leaves of the White Oak are as large as a squirrel's foot. When the Blackberry is in full bloom, all danger of frost is past and all the rest may be safely planted.

Country Proverbs.

The HERBARIST *for* 1942

A Limited Edition
Written and Published by
THE HERB SOCIETY *of* AMERICA

PRICE $1.00
(If ordering by mail, please allow 2 cents postage per copy)

A few copies of previous years are still available
at $1.00 each

Other Publications of The Herb Society *of* America

THE STILL HOUSE. Booklet. 1935.	.25
COMPLEAT COURT-COOK-1716 Excerpts from (1937)	.10
PLACE OF THE DRIED HERB IN INDUSTRY. Leaflet (1937)	.05
BELLADONNA-Reprint from Herbarist, (1941)	.25
LIST OF GARDENS AND HERBARIA DEVOTED TO MEDICINAL AND OTHER HERBS. (1941)	.15
NOTES ON COMMERCIAL CULTIVATION OF SAGE. Jan. (1941)	.15
RECORDS OF A GROUP OF SAGE GROWERS. Jan. (1942)	.25
FERTILIZER TEST ON SAGE. (1942) Leaflet.	.05

IN Preparation: THE HOME HERB GARDEN.

Address
THE HERB SOCIETY *of* AMERICA
HORTICULTURAL HALL
300 Massachusetts Avenue   Boston, Massachusetts

AN HERB PRIMER
by G. M. BROWN
TOPSFIELD, MASS.

New and revised edition   50 cents

Order from J. B. Pierce, Topsfield, Mass.

The HERBARIST *for* 1942

A Limited Edition
Written and Published by
THE HERB SOCIETY *of* AMERICA

PRICE $1.00
(If ordering by mail, please allow 2 cents postage per copy)

A few copies of previous years are still available
at $1.00 each

Other Publications of The Herb Society *of* America

THE STILL HOUSE. Booklet. 1935.	.25
COMPLEAT COURT-COOK-1716 Excerpts from (1937)	.10
PLACE OF THE DRIED HERB IN INDUSTRY. Leaflet (1937)	.05
BELLADONNA-Reprint from Herbarist, (1941)	.25
LIST OF GARDENS AND HERBARIA DEVOTED TO MEDICINAL AND OTHER HERBS. (1941)	.15
NOTES ON COMMERCIAL CULTIVATION OF SAGE. Jan. (1941)	.15
RECORDS OF A GROUP OF SAGE GROWERS. Jan. (1942)	.25
FERTILIZER TEST ON SAGE. (1942) Leaflet.	.05

IN Preparation: THE HOME HERB GARDEN.

Address
THE HERB SOCIETY *of* AMERICA
HORTICULTURAL HALL
300 Massachusetts Avenue   Boston, Massachusetts

AN HERB PRIMER
by G. M. BROWN
TOPSFIELD, MASS.

~•◎•~

New and revised edition   50 *cents*

Order from J. B. Pierce, Topsfield, Mass.

MAGIC IN HERBS
By LEONIE DE SOUNIN
Introduction by MIRIAM BIRDSEYE

A glorious new book for the gourmet and gardener. Mouth-watering recipes and menus capture the essence of the herb. You will learn a tradition of herb gardening and herb cooking from the aristocrat of a fine old European culture who has given us the secrets of her ancestral cuisine. Send for a copy now, ten-day return privilege. Illustrated. $2.00 at bookstores or from

M. BARROWS & CO., Inc.
443 Fourth Avenue   New York

HERBS
FROM
THE LITTLE HOUSE
ANNISQUAM, MASS.

PLANTS - DRIED HERBS

SEND FOR FREE CATALOG

HERBS

HERB PLANTS: pot grown, easily shipped: spring, summer and fall.

DRIED HERBS: home-grown, dated, carefully prepared, single ingredients as well as our own popular blends for Salads, Omelets, Soups, Poultry Stuffing, Tomato Recipes, Sauces, etc.

HERB COOKERY: attractive Booklet, just published, with excellent Recipes for Herbs, sent on receipt of 25 cents.

HERB CATALOGUE: listing over 100 varieties, with cultural directions, etc., sent on receipt of 10 cents.

WEATHERED OAK HERB FARM, Inc.
Bradley Hills, Bethesda, Maryland

CHARLES H. MERRYMAN
President and General Manager

When you come to
WILLIAMSBURG, VIRGINIA,
as all the world is now doing, you will enjoy visiting

THE HERB & GARDEN SHOP

in its attractive setting which reflects the charm of this Colonial City. Do come in to see us.

THE HERB & GARDEN SHOP
Specialists in Culinary Herbs
on Nicholson Street near the Colonial Gaol in Williamsburg, Virginia

---

HERB PLANTS
New England Grown for Northern Gardens

100 varieties
and
Sweet-Leaved
Geraniums

Catalogue on request
HIGHMEAD NURSERY, INC.
Dept. 9
IPSWICH, MASS.

Second Printing

Herbs

How to Grow Them and How to Use Them

By HELEN NOYES WEBSTER

Complete — Practical — Low-Priced

Here you will find famous plans of herb gardens: lists for planting period gardens and for herb families; the herbs to use in modern gardens; valuable information about the use of herbs: and of course complete cultural information. Written by one of the country's leading authorities, it will make it easy to have an herb garden that will be a delight to you and the envy of your friends.

160 pages - - - 36 illustrations, Octavo only, $1.00.   Postpaid in U. S.

Make checks payable to

HORTICULTURE, Horticultural Hall, Boston, Mass.

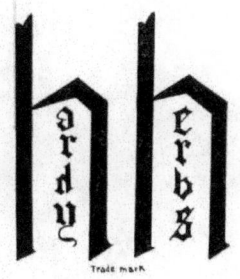

Culinary-dried herb combinations
Herb Vinegars
Horehound Candy

SHERMAN K. and VERA B. HARDY
EIGHTY HILL STREET   LEXINGTON, MASS.

ORIGINATORS of the HERB-BAR

HERB CHEST
$1.50

For the Young Bride or the Housewife

A red tin box containing 9 envelopes of herbs and a chart of directions.

Herbs include basil, bay leaves, chervil, marjoram, mint, rosemary, sage, tarragon, thyme.

S. S. PIERCE CO.
133 Brookline Avenue
Boston

A New Exciting Product
from
SAW MILL FARM

Charleston Sauce

A unique seasoning for meats, salads, cheese dishes, sea-food and eggs.

SENT POSTPAID
55c
with a list of our 50

HERBRIETIES
Reg. U. S. Pat. Off.

Delicious, unusual herbed foods garden-fresh herbs and blends.

Order from
MARCIA GARRICK
SAW MILL FARM
New City,   Rockland County, New York

•

"FARE ON THE FARM"
A provocative, informative booklet
25 cents

The HERBARIST

A Publication of
The Herb Society of America

No. 9

For Use and for Delight

BOSTON, MASSACHUSETTS

1943

Newcomb & Gauss Co., Printers
Salem, Massachusetts

Copyright, 1943, by the Herb Society of America

CONTENTS

	PAGE
FRONTISPIECE: The Adoration of the Child	4
By Giovanni Battista Utili	
FOREWORD	5
PORCHER, MEDICAL BOTANIST IN A TIME OF NEED	
Colonel Edgar Erskine Hume, U. S. A.	8
ANGELICA: An Etching by Caroline Weir Ely	12
ANGELICA ARCHANGELICA Mrs. Arthur B. Baer	13
SOME UNUSUAL POT-HERBS Helen Morgenthau Fox	18
OLD AMERICAN WOODEN WARE	23
Photographs by Mary Earle Gould	
NEW USES FOR FAMILIAR AMERICAN PLANTS	
Compiled by the Editors	23
THE GROWING OF HERBS IN WAR TIME	27
THE COTTAGE GARDEN HERB INDUSTRY	
Sherman K. and Vera B. Hardy	29
"TWELVE BASKETS FULL" Frances R. Williams	36
AN IMPORTANT ADDITION TO AMERICANA	39
FROM MAINE AND ALL ALONGSHORE — IRISH MOSS	42
EXPERIMENTS BY NEW ENGLAND MEMBERS	45
Belladonna — Digitalis — Ramie	
ENGLAND'S KITCHEN FRONT	48
FIELD NOTES	51
OUR CONTRIBUTORS	54
THE HERB SOCIETY OF AMERICA: Officers and Directors	56

THE ADORATION OF THE CHILD WITH SAINTS AND DONORS
By Giovanni Battista Utili (Kress Collection, National Gallery)

In the foreground, painted with the delicate accuracy of a Persian miniature, the following plants can be easily recognized: aquilegia, strawberry, mint, oxalis, parsley, pimpernel, woodruff, burnet, dianthus, sorrel, arrow root, dandelion and vinca.

Courtesy of the National Gallery of Art, Washington, D. C.

FOREWORD

EMERGING from the cataclysm of this second world war, we can already see economic as well as social changes which promise to revolutionize our living. The harnessing of the research laboratory to the farm is bringing from the earth, even from its wastes, products and plants to supply pressing needs. The Department of Agriculture, suddenly called upon to face unprecedented conditions and to supply lacking commodities on a grand scale, has established a great stand of guayule in California, private research laboratories have created new textiles and plastics, growers have grown new plants and improved old varieties, so that the year 1942 has seen great progress. Textiles, oil and rubber are all products of the land which the United States and its Allies can grow and supply.

Many articles of commerce in the past have had the common denominator of cheap labor. In the future, that denominator may be changed to mass production, co-operatives, machinery. Does this mean that our years of effort to revive and re-establish the herb-growing industry are all lost energy? We submit that private initiative may make an important contribution of its own, not only during the war years but in the time of reconstruction afterward. The farmer, instead of fighting for parity or appropriations, may find at his door the opportunity to grow the products for which the laboratory has found a new use and for which there is a new market. Land owners have a special obligation to grow needed foodstuffs up to the point where they can control sufficient labor to harvest and market their product.

The scarcity of two of our most important drug plants has focussed attention on that oldest of medical sources, the plant kingdom. While it is not the province of the layman to enter the medical field, there still remain ways in which our members with a serious purpose can be useful. It is not stepping too far into the sacred precincts of the medical profession to undertake some preliminary studies; the folk-lore of the medical uses of plants, if we may call it so, is a wide research field, as is the study of the old herbals. It should not be forgotten that the use of digitalis as a heart tonic was the contribution of a layman to medical science. Healing by plants and herbs is one of the most ancient of skills, and while some of these ancient cure-alls were fakes, many others were potent in combating disease and suffering, and many are still essential. Every great advance in chemistry and medicine shows how little is known even yet of these mysterious plant materials, and a vital job of the present is the finding of plant sources and learning how to increase them. This may well fall to the lot of the layman, while to the laboratory must be referred the task of getting the plant principles from the raw materials. The laboratories of Eli Lilly, E. R. Squibb & Sons, Merck & Co., and others are active in this research.

The demands of the war with its higher paid jobs have produced an acute lack of labor and reduce the number of collectors of the wild material which is the source of our home remedies—the tried and true familiars of the cupboard of the rural inhabitant, or the ingredients of patent medicines. Of our drug supplies, 55% came from European or Far Eastern countries, where most of them grow wild. Introduced to cultivation in different soil they sometimes lose their characteristics, and here is another opportunity for the private grower: experimental plots and a study of soil and environment, with the co-operation of the chemist to determine the value of the new-grown plant. The continued experiments with belladonna by members of the Herb Society, reported upon in this number, are in line with this effort.

The present high prices paid for herbs have tempted many to undertake the growing of this new crop, with the understanding that such prices will not prevail after the scarcity has been alleviated. But these growers will have gained a knowledge of the growing and preparation for market, a technique in drying the product, a familiarity with their subject which will remain a distinct asset for the future. With the experience of these years we may still develop this minor crop as profitable for crop diversification. It would seem a short-sighted policy on the part of our government authorities to hold back the herb-growing industry in order to control the postwar international trade, and thereby choking off a growing domestic industry.

Our best and greatest contribution as a Society, therefore, is to do the thing we know best, taking up what we find closest at hand and giving our time and labor and the resources of our gardens and libraries to amplifying the knowledge of useful plants. We shall have earned a place in the ranks of the war-workers and who knows but that another layman may stumble upon some happy discovery which will merit the praise of the professionals.

PORCHER, MEDICAL BOTANIST
IN A TIME OF NEED

EDGAR ERSKINE HUME
Colonel, Medical Corps, U. S. Army

IF there is anything good about wars it is the way they have of making folk do the things that must be done, using only the things that can be had. There can be none of the practice of pampering specialists and highly skilled workers, too many of whom merely shrug their shoulders and decline to work if they have not their favorite tools, their special brands of materials, and the exact working conditions that they desire. Americans are learning anew what they have had to learn in all our major wars—that the job must be done, and when the best materials are not to hand, then with the best that are available.

In the terrible War Between the States, 1861-1865, the Union Army was often unable to obtain all the supplies that it needed. For instance, cotton, tobacco, sugar, and other supplies were insufficient. But the North was rich indeed in comparison with the South where there was a dearth of nearly all manufactured articles and of everything that had to be imported. The shortage that caused the most suffering was the lack of medicines and medical supplies. Many a soldier, including prisoners from the North, died because quinine was a contraband of war, to cite one example.

The American spirit of carrying on even under the most adverse conditions was nowhere better demonstrated than in the Medical Department of the Confederate Army. Some of the things accomplished arouse our highest admiration in these times when our sick and wounded men want for nothing. The Surgeon General, Samuel Preston Moore of South Carolina, is one of the remarkable figures of American military medicine. He did so much with so little. Not the least of his claims to lasting fame was his selection of a fellow South Carolinian, Francis Peyre Porcher (1825-1895) to supply medicinal plants and the products made therefrom. Porcher, moreover, had the far harder task of supplying substitute plants, when the ones desired could not be had. He was a man who would be most useful to Hitler and his minions right now!

Porcher, the son of a physician, was one of the group of Huguenots whose ancestors came to South Carolina after the Revocation of the Edict of Nantes. He received his academic training at South Carolina College and his medical degree from the Medical College of South Carolina (1847). Subsequently he rounded out his training by two years' study in Paris and some months in Italy.

Early interested in botany, he published *A Sketch of Medical Botany of South Carolina* in 1849, being not yet twenty-four years of age. Thereafter he took a leading part in medical progress in his native State. He assisted in the establishment of the Charleston Preparatory Medical School, served for many years on the Board of Health, and as clinical professor in the Medical College, being at the same time physician and surgeon in the several Charleston hospitals. In 1852 he traveled extensively in Europe, contributing accounts of his experiences to the *Charleston Medical Journal and Review*, for which he also translated a number of French and Italian articles.

He achieved national reputation as a medical botanist by his paper *The Medicinal, Poisonous and Dietetic Properties of the Cryptogamic Plants of the United States*, which he read before the American Medical Association in 1854. Thus we find the background for his selection by the Surgeon General as the one man who might give the Confederate Army medicines of plant origin.

Porcher was ever a skilful clinician and humanitarian. In 1855, with Dr. John Julian Chisholm, he opened in Charleston a hospital for Negroes, designed especially to care for slaves from the plantations, where accomodations for the care of such patients were wanting. During the war he served in various capacities as a military surgeon, such as with the Holcombe Legion, at the Naval Hospital at Norfolk, and the South Carolina Hospital at Petersburg, Virginia.

But it is as a botanist that he is chiefly remembered. In 1863, he published *The Resources of the Southern Fields and Forests,* a volume of several hundred pages, of which Paul Hamilton Hayne said that it justified Porcher "a national and European reputation." The monograph was revised in 1869, and war being over, was available to scientists of the whole country. Porcher distributed copies to many libraries, desiring no financial reward for his work. One of these copies was sent to his old friend, Surgeon General Joseph K. Barnes, U. S. Army, with a letter dated Charleston, 24 November 1869, saying: "I hope upon examination you will find [it] a useful work. If you have no special use for it in your Department, please deposit for me in the Library which it has been proposed to establish in Washington for American works.... I have had to distribute a great many copies and publish the work myself." Barnes placed the book in the Army Medical Library (then known as the Library of the Surgeon General's Office), where it remains one of the treasures of this, the largest medical library on earth.

Porcher's reputation was international. He held membership in many important American and European learned societies, and was one of the organizers of the Associaton of American Physicians. In 1890 he was one of ten delegates on the part of the United States to the tenth international Medical Congress in Berlin, and in the following year was the only American delegate to a similar congress in Rome. He was a prolific writer on medical and botanical subjects.

In the "Preliminary" to the second edition of his great monograph he says: "The first edition was prepared during the late war by direction of the Surgeon-General of the Confederate

States, that the Medical Officers, as well as the public might be supplied with the information which, at that time, was greatly needed." He adds that his goal was "to throw light upon the vegetable productions of the Southern States, to enable everyone to use the abundant material within his reach." The book contains minute directions for the collection, drying, and preparation of medicinal plants. It also gives certain simple tests by which the active principles of medicinal plants may be recognized and their strength determined. The technique of wine making is given likewise, this being not only in itself a medicine but the solvent for many medicines. There is also not a little information as to antidotes for plant poisons, lists of active principles which must not be used together, those which work in harmony, and the like. Space precludes a detailed account of Porcher's famous book, but one does not have to be a botanist to realize in looking it over that it was a mighty attempt to solve a problem of first urgency, an attempt that was largely successful.

Cress in the House.—A bit of fresh green as a welcome addition to the midwinter diet is easily obtained by growing Cress in a sunny window. The best variety of seed is the Extra Curled or Pepper Grass, and if sprinkled over the top of coarse wet sand in a discarded goldfish bowl or aquarium with a glass lid, it will germinate in a few days.

ANGELICA—An Etching *by Caroline Weir Ely*

ANGELICA ARCHANGELICA
MRS. ARTHUR B. BAER

"Angelica, the happy counter bane
 Sent down from heaven by some celestial scout
 As well its name and nature both avow't."
  Du Bartes: Sylvester's Translation, 1641.

IF Angelica were so virtuous what must Archangelica be? Why the plant first received these names is not altogether certain, but the popular explanation is that it was so called from its well known good qualities. Perhaps the latter name refers to St. Michael the Archangel, whose day falls on the Eighth of May (old style) when the flower would be in bloom and consequently was supposed to be a preservative against witchcraft.

Parkinson in his "Theatrum Botanicum" points out that all Christian nations call the plant by names signifying its angelic associations, and "likewise in their appelations hereof follow the Latine name as near as their Dialect will permit only in Sussex they call the wild kind Kex, and the weavers wind their yarne on the dead stalks." The Laplanders crowned their poets with it, believing that the odour inspired them, and they also thought that the use of it "strengthens life." They chew and smoke it in the same way as tobacco. The Letts endowed Angelica with magical powers, and the songs which are chanted by them when the herb is carried to market are very ancient.

The natural habitat of Angelica is Scotland, East Prussia, Iceland, Lapland and Syria. Before the war it was grown commercially in Germany (Thuringia and Saxony), in England, Poland, Russia, Belgium, Italy and France. It is cultivated extensively near Clermont-Ferrand in France for making liqueurs.

It is supposed to have come to this country in 1568. Angelica was mentioned as being in Adrian Van der Donck's garden

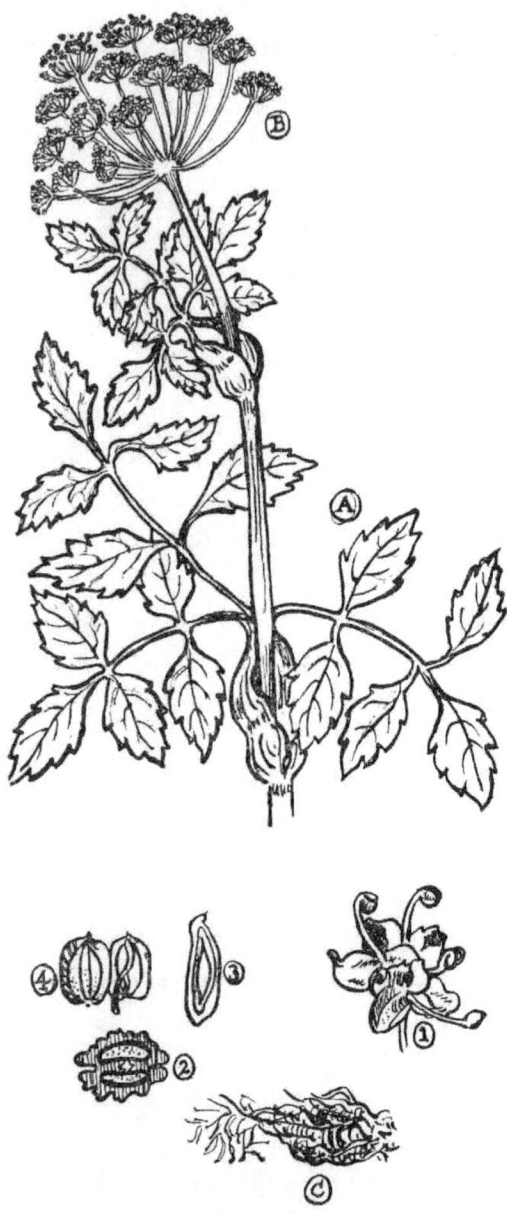

ANGELICA
(*Angelica Archangelica* L.)

A. Leafy shoot.
B. Inflorescence
C. Rhizome and roots
1. Flower
2. Cross-Section of fruit
3. Mature carpel showing single seed
4. Mature fruits.

at Yonkers in 1653. This was perhaps the native Angelica Atropurpurea. Angelica seed listed as A. purpurea was offered for sale in the advertisements of the Boston Evening Post in 1771, and by Bertram in 1814.

Of all the Angelicas, and there are around fifty of them in the northern hemisphere, only two are likely subjects in the American herb garden: A. Archangelica, the cultivated Angelica, and A. atropurpurea, the wild American species sometimes known as Masterwort. They are lusty fellows, grown in the rich moist soil they love, spending a youthful year or so to develop into a rosette of leaves and a parsnip-like root, and then in a single season dramatically bursting up six to ten feet high to flower, set seed and die. Their leaves, rather like a cruder celery leaf, rise from bulbous bases so wide that they encircle the hollow stem. The flowers are small, but they are bunched in tight little pompoms and groups of these pompoms are compounded into a large sunburst. This whole inflorescence is technically known as an umbel of umbels, or a compound umbel, a dull enough name for such a fascinating structure, which in its main line resembles a bursting sky-rocket.

In flower, in leaf, and in general habit these two species of Angelica are very much alike and rather different from most of the other species of the genus. For one thing they are smooth-stemmed and smooth-leaved, as smooth as celery, while many of the other species are more or less hairy. The garden A. Archangelica differs from its American cousin A. atropurpurea in being a little less coarse, much less highly colored, and in having a more delicate aroma. The American species has a rank medicinal odour, the European a delicate and attractive one strongly reminiscent of Benedictine and similar liqueurs.

Angelica belongs to one of the most distinctive of the great plant families, the Umbelliferae, the "umbel bearers," as do also dill, borage, chervil, parsley and other lesser herbs. The leaves all possess the same pattern, being more or less cut as the case may be. Through the whole family there runs a very similar set of odors and flavours; the flowers are similar throughout too, having a yellow-greenish color. The fruit, called seeds, are 6-7 mm. in diameter and greenish in color with five visible striations.

Angelica is biennial only in the botanical sense of that term: that is to say, it is neither annual nor perennial. The seedlings make but little advance toward maturity within twelve months, while old plants die off after seeding once, which may be at a more remote period than in the second year of growth. Only very advanced seedlings flower in their second year, and the third year commonly completes the full period of life. If the flower heads are cut before seeding the plants can last many years.

Angelica can be raised by seeding in the usual manner, but germination is apt to be slow and irregular. It is best to store the seeds as they ripen (in July and August), in moist sand for several weeks before sowing. Seeds are sown in rows 11.8 inches apart with a distance of 24 to 28 inches between rows. Sowing may also be accomplished through the use of small pieces of root. Turning and layering the topsoil is the practice used to prevent weed growth; the seeds are not damaged by these procedures because they are deeply planted, 7 or 8 inches. In order to produce a more aromatic root, the tops of the plant are cut off to prevent formation of seed. Angelica grows best in a moderate climate, in good soil, preferably with a deep layer of moist clay. It likes, too, a partially shaded spot. It should be planted on a fresh site every few years as it deteriorates rapidly if grown in the same soil too long. It requires 8 to 11 pounds of seed per acre.

The harvesting season for roots is in the spring (April), or fall (September or October), and seeds are also harvested in the fall. After one year of growth the root is carefully harvested, washed and dried by air. It is advised to keep roots ready for sale in closed containers to protect them against loss of aroma and also against insects. The crop yield is from 900 to 1300 pounds per acre.

Essential oil is distributed throughout the whole plant, being found in the seeds, leaves, stems and roots. Commercially, the important parts are the roots, then seeds, and stems.

Angelica is largely used in the grocery trade and for medicine, and is popular as a flavouring for confectionery and liqueurs. The appreciation of its flavour was established in olden times when saccharin matter was extremely rare. Formerly the leaf-stalks were blanched and eaten like celery, but now they are candied. In the 16th, 17th and 18th centuries Angelica leaves were candied as well; the roots were made into preserves, and Angelica water was a favorite cordial. The flavor suggests that of juniper berries, and it is largely used with juniper berries or in partial substitution for them by gin distillers. The seeds especially, which are aromatic and bitterish in taste, are also employed in alcoholic distillates.

Medicinally speaking, the root, stalk, leaves and fruit possess carminative, stimulate, diaphoretic, tonic and expectorant properties, which are strongest in the fruit, though the whole plant has the same virtues. A remedy given in an old family herbal for hoarseness, sore throat or coughs is as follows: Boil down gently for 3 hours a handful of Angelica root in a quart of water, then strain it off and add to liquid narbonne honey (honey from thymes and mints) or best Virgin honey sufficient to make it into a balsam or syrup, add a few drops of nitre, and take.... several times a day.

Angelica may be cut into pieces and candied in sugar syrup for a confection. Another recipe is for Rhubarb and Angelica jam: Cut rhubarb into inch-length pieces; weigh and allow ¾ lb. sugar to each pound of rhubarb. Put in a kettle with sugar, a little lemon piece, and a few tender stalks of Angelica cut into small pieces. Cook down to a thick jam, stirring frequently. Put in glasses and seal.

SOME UNUSUAL POT-HERBS
HELEN MORGENTHAU FOX

THESE days, all over the world, people are looking for food that can be supplied with the least labor and provide a high vitamin and mineral content. Consequently greens not well known to the general public will be a welcome addition to the garden. Among these are edible weeds that have been eaten down through the ages. Some of them are exceedingly tasty and it is surprising that they have not been featured more in cook books. Another group of almost forgotten vegetables are some of the perennial greens. The only care they require is weeding and dividing. Six to eight plants of perennials, such as sorrel or comfrey, and a dozen of chicory, will supply the needs of the average family of four or six.

A few of the plants hitherto grown for flavor provide delicious pot-herbs. Such a one is borage, generally grown for the flowering tops to impart flavor of cucumber to fruit drinks and wine cups. The leaves are hairy, but as happens with many greens, they lose this during the cooking. Only the young, tender leaves are palatable. Borage is a weed along the Mediterranean shores and when it grows in citrous orchards the blue flowers are handsome with the yellow and orange fruits above them. Borage grows in any garden soil, and a little bed of it, 4 x 8 feet, is large enough for the needs of one family. It can be sown for the first time when the maples are in flower and again four weeks later, and will self-sow a third time for an autumn crop.

Off to one side of the garden where they can remain undisturbed when the other beds are being ploughed, can be plantings of perennial vegetables. Most of the leaves are edible only when young and tender. The earliest green to come up, often through the snow, is sorrel, *Rumex Acetosa*. The leaves can be used either in salads, for soups, or to mix with other pot-herbs to which they give their acid, mouth-puckering flavor. Sorrel increases rapidly through underground stolons and must be divided every second year or oftener. From the wild plant several cultivated varieties have been developed. A form called *Oseille de Belleville,* or broad-leaved French, has pale broad leaves, less acid than the type. In American markets sorrel with upright leaves is favored.

Recipe—a version of Soupe a la Bonne Femme.

Ingredients: 2 cups milk, 1 cup stock, 1 teaspoon salt, 2 tablespoons butter or other shortening, 2 tablespoons flour, 1 medium sized onion, 1 cup finely chopped sorrel, ½ cup cream, 2 egg yolks.

Melt shortening, add flour, salt, the liquids and onion. Boil for 1 hour. Remove the onion, add ½ cup cream mixed with yolks of 2 eggs. Cook until thickened. Just before serving add either ½ cup finely chopped parsley, sorrel, or Chinese mustard or water cress, stir well and serve at once. (From Fox, "Gardening with Herbs," with some changes).

A perennial related to borage, and having a similar cucumber flavor, is comfrey, *Symphytum officinale,* with the additional popular names of consolida, knit-bone and gum plant. Comfrey comes from Europe and temperate Asia, is a hardy perennial and grows two feet high. The leaves are roughly hairy, about seven inches long and three across, pointed, and grow in lusty clumps. The flowers are red-to-violet, tubular, hang in pendulous clusters and are small in relation to the leaves. In the past, comfrey was valued as a vulnerary. When the young leaves are cooked in an open kettle with a goodly amount of water they make a delicious, somewhat rich if slightly coarse-textured green. Formerly the roots were cooked, but roots of plants grown in my New York State garden are bitter and astringent.

Recipe—Herb Pie.

Ingredients: 2 handfuls parsley leaves, 2 handfuls spinach,

2 lettuces, 2 handfuls cress or Chinese mustard, a few leaves of borage and comfrey, and a handful of beet leaves, 2 eggs, ¾ cup cream, ¼ cup milk.

Wash and boil the leaves a little. Then drain and press out the water, cut them small, mix and lay in a baking dish and sprinkle with salt. Add 2 eggs beaten, ¾ cup cream, ¼ cup milk, all mixed, and stir into greens. Cover the mixture with a crust, as for pie, and bake for 20 minutes until crust is brown. (From Fox, "Gardening for Good Eating.")

This dish tastes of a combination of cucumber and parsley and is delightful for lunch.

Though Good King Henry, *Chenopodium Bonus-Henricus*, is said to be perennial and last for several seasons, I have found it behaves as an annual. It is native in Europe and has escaped a little in North Eastern America. Seeds are sown in a seed-bed early in spring and the seedlings are transferred to the garden and planted two feet apart each way. The round stems are semi-recumbent, about 18 inches long, and the leaves arrow-shaped with two fairly long lobes. According to seventeenth century cook books, besides eating the leaves, the young shoots that had first been blanched were peeled and cooked. When steamed in very little water, the leaves taste slightly bitter and have an oily quality, so much so that no shortening needs to be added to them to make them palatable.

A hardy perennial as yet little known in America, though highly popular in England, is *Crambe Maritima*, sea-kale, or scurvy grass. Sea-kale grows along the European coasts of the Atlantic Ocean and has been known to sailors since Roman days. They gathered and packed the leaves in barrels to take on long sea voyages, thus providing themselves with vitamins without knowing the scientific explanations. The plant grows three feet high and has large, thick leaves similar to the cabbage to which it is related. The English, who forced sea-kale for the first time in the seventeenth century, have perfected an elaborate culture to induce the plant to produce tender shoots and have special pots for covering them. In the absence of these pots the plants, three feet apart each way, can be hilled one foot or more with earth. A good crop cannot be expected before the plants are two to three years old.

Selected forms of the straggly weed with charming blue flowers, chicory, *Cichorium intybus,* provide young leaves for salads, or pot-herbs during hot weather. In fall the roots can be dug and planted with their tops eight inches below the soil in hotbeds, cold frames, a greenhouse, or a kitchen window and forced to provide greens all winter. Chicory is perennial, and forms with wider and less bitter leaves than wild plants are called witloof, French endive, or Brussels chicory. Unless they are forced the leaves are bitter tasting but are pleasing to many and can be eaten either alone or mixed with blandly tasting greens.

Though frequently grown in Europe, seeds of orach, mountain spinach, or butter leaves, *Atriplex hortensis,* are difficult as yet to locate in this country. Orach comes from Central Asia and Siberia and is said to be the oldest cultivated plant. It is a tall hardy annual reaching $2\frac{1}{2}$ feet. The arrow-shaped, puckery leaves grow on long stalks and have toothed and wavy margins. They continue to produce tender and palatable leaves if the stems are cut back every now and then. There are several forms and the one most frequently planted has pale green leaves. The best way to prepare orach leaves is to steam them in very little water; the texture of the cooked leaves is soft and the flavor pleasant.

Those who have no vegetable gardens can have a supply of fresh greens rich in vitamins all through the growing season by gathering weeds along roads, in meadows, swamps and forests. It is a reckless gardener who would introduce purslane, pusley, in Latin *Portulaca oleracea,* into the garden if the seed is not already thickly scattered through the top soil. There is a cultivated form, called var. *sativa,* more erect than the wild, and a form with yellow leaves. When raw, purslane has a lightly acid taste and is crisp and pleasant in salads; when cooked it feels as green air might in the mouth. To cook them, leaves and tops are dropped into boiling salted water and left ten minutes after the water has begun to boil again. The plants shrink to less than half their bulk in cooking.

Collecting Lamb's Quarters, *Chenopodium album,* as with purslane, helps eradicate a troublesome weed. The plant is annual, and looks gray. The stems, if undisturbed, are said to attain ten feet in height. The leaves are trowel-shaped, pointed and toothed, and the flowers nondescript, green, and grow in loose panicles. Lamb's quarters have been eaten since prehistoric times in Europe and America where the Indians ate both leaves and tops as well as seeds. In cooking, the first water is discarded because of the unpleasant taste; the young leaves are then boiled for 20 minutes, and when served taste of garden fragrance.

It was a pleasant surprise to find the leaves of the coarse weed, red root, *Amaranthus retroflexus,* provide a tender pot-herb with a distinctive, delicate flavor and oily quality. The stems are cerise above the ground and below it into the root and have been reported as high as 10 feet. The leaves are rounded at the tips, somewhat triangular, and the flowers are crowded into stiff, terminal, spiny clusters. American Indians cultivate red root for the seed, high in protein and starch.

Any of these greens can be cooked exactly like spinach either alone or blended with other greens. A recipe for pot-herbs follows:

Greens with Bacon: Ingredients, 2 pounds of greens, a little pepper, salt, 6 slices of bacon. Cook the greens; when tender, chop and season, add bacon that has been cooked until crisp and cut into small pieces. A small amount of lemon juice can also be added. (From Fox, "Gardening for Good Eating.")

A Gathering-tray, Mortar and Pestle, Horse-hair Sieves and Boxes used for Herbal Remedies, from an Old-Time Doctor's Equipment.

Courtesy of Mary Earle Gould

NEW USES for FAMILIAR AMERICAN PLANTS*

THE American farmer may be entering upon a new era holding promise which seems almost limitless. As new experiments in chemistry and chemurgy with familiar materials follow each other, it would seem as if agriculture had been forever shaken

(*Notes gathered from The Chemurgic Digest, commercial and market reports and other sources. Ed.)

out of its humdrum ways and was assuming vast new significance.

Mr. Henry Ford, whose word on mechanical subjects commands respect, says:

"You will see the time when a good many automobile parts will be grown. The engine, drive shaft and other driving and structural parts will of course be made of metal, but much of the rest, including the body, will be made of farm products."

In support of this, we find that the Ford Plant has a program already under way looking toward growing substitutes for rubber, lubricants, fabric materials and accessories. Molasses from 12,500 acres of cane went into anti-freeze and shock absorbers. Cotton for safety glass and brake-linings, soybean oil for making a lustrous and long-wearing enamel and several fiber plants for heavy upholstery fabrics are the results of other new processes.

Wood Waste—An experiment at the University of New Hampshire is discovering uses for wood waste, the slash from forest cutting, and mill sawdust which heretofore has been burned; a plastic molding powder is being developed which because of the low cost of production may be produced in great quantity to be applied to wall board, veneer base, window-frames, etc. Another waste which for years has been allowed to flow down New Hampshire's rivers is lignin, or the natural cementing material which binds wood fibers together and which is dissolved at high temperature and washed out. This is now found capable of conversion into a good plastic material.

Grasses—Tender blades of oats, wheat, barley, rye and sudan grasses which have been scientifically grown and cut in an early stage of growth are found to yield a maximum of nutriment. These unjointed grasses must be cut before the first joint is formed when the plant is tender, green and succulent. The plant is exerting itself to joint and reproduce and is consequently at the peak of its stored-up energy; afterwards it becomes fibrous and woody. The mixture grown under ideal conditions of sun and irrigation contains hormone-like factors which make it a marvellous poultry food, and research is being applied to making it suitable for human nutrition as well.

Oil Plants—Experiments show that Safflower is one of the most promising new oil crops. Mustard oil has long been used in medicines, but it is also reported to be a competitor of cottonseed oil for special industrial purposes. Peppermint has been chiefly marketed as a flavoring and a source of menthol, but new therapeutic uses for it have now been found. Laurel (umbelluria Californica) is reported to be an untapped source of thymol and tannin, two products of which our market is very short. Soybean oil has many uses in commerce, besides being full of protein, and is now an ingredient of a new water paint. Grape seeds are a source of oil for leather and textile finishing.

Fiber Plants—As our supply of Manila hemp from the Philippines and other places has fallen off, the search for a first class substitute goes on. The following plants are listed by Robert W. Schery of the Missouri Botanical Garden: New Zealand hemp (grown in California), Flax, Ramie, Milkweed, Dogbane. Of these the most promising is said to be milkweed, only exceeded by Manila hemp in both breaking and tensile strength. A difficulty here is that a farmer would hesitate to plant milkweed in any quantity unless guaranteed beforehand of his market; its nuisance quality as an "escape" would be considerable.

Miscellaneous—Cattails, ordinarily looked upon as a rank growth in swamps, are now being gathered as a source of insulating materials. If this develops as an industry, many acres now worthless will be made productive. Corn stalks, whose fiber is of poor quality, may supply valuable cellulose. Milkweed seed-hairs provide a good substitute for Kapok in life-preservers and jackets, being impervious to water.

With all these new and quite individual materials, their market value must wait on the introduction of new machinery for processing. Several years may be needed to work out the handling, and at present new machinery is scarcely obtainable. Seed must also be made available to growers after the best sorts have been proved.

Essential Oils—Here, on the other hand, it seems that a market is waiting. The cutting down of imports has produced a great shortage of essential oils, and America has been getting substitutes from coal tar and derivatives; so far the development of the oil industry has been limited. Many oils were developed in Russia, the chief sources being plants easily grown here, such as angelica, anise, birch, caraway, celery, coriander, fennel, hyssop, iris, juniper berry, lavender, lovage, marjoram, thyme, wormwood. With a large acreage of cheap land and with machine labor to keep production costs low, this could soon become an important American industry. There has already been a 20% increase in peppermint acreage for obtaining domestic menthol.

Improved Methods—Much valuable material can be conserved by careful methods. Oil is lost in the wastage of broken leaves. Last year R. H. Wileman, an agricultural engineer of Purdue University, designed and made a machine to pick up shattered leaves, and an average of 3 pounds per acre was salvaged from such leaves. Farmers are also learning that the careful weeding of the fields before harvest and the strict cleanliness of all machinery and containers will prevent the discoloration that means an offgrade product.

THE GROWING OF HERBS IN WAR TIME
THE COMMERCIAL RESEARCH COMMITTEE

THE Herb Society of America is constantly faced with the question, "What do you advise? We have the land, we want to help—what shall we grow?" This is a sincere and patriotic inquiry which merits an equally sincere and honest reply.

In order to clarify the confusion which has been produced by the publication of articles which lack the background of basic fact and experience, the Herb Society urges these prospective growers to consider carefully the very clearly defined divisions of herb growing. These divisions are quite different in their requirements, methods and objectives.

1. MEDICINAL HERBS

a. The growing of medicinal herbs should not be undertaken by the novice, even though a shortage exists caused by war conditions.

b. Medicinal crops require more than growing. Harvesting, drying and marketing of a crop more specialized than other crops demands expert knowledge and experience.

2. CONDIMENT HERBS

a. Home growing of the kitchen herbs, for home use. Every encouragement should be given to the undertaking of this division of herb growing. No class of horticultural endeavor gives more satisfaction than a kitchen herb patch for practical use, and it can play a real part in the education of the public taste. This small start also can help to determine if expansion into an industry is practical. Twelve herbs are advised as a start. (See Bulletin on Home Growing, Herb Society of America.)

b. Cottage Industry—for retail selling. Expansion of the herb patch into a larger area. This requires experience not only in growing and drying but in processing for use and packing for retail business. It is not sufficient to put on the market a unique container; the contents must conform to recognized standards for color and potency.

c. Commercial Growing—for wholesale trade. The commercial grower should be a good farmer; seed and fertilizer should not be wasted by poor growers. The grower must have sufficient available labor. He must have adequate drying facilities. He must be familiar with the requirements of the trade, and he must be assured of his market. The grower should have supervision the first year, if unfamiliar with his crop. Information is limited as to culture, costs and yield in different sections of the country. (See Bulletin, Experiences of Some New England Growers of Sage in 1941, Herb Society of America.)

3. SCIENTIFIC RESEARCH

Experimental plots can be of great service if the cost of development need not be considered. Information is needed as to culture, reaction to soil, times of harvesting, different methods of drying. Such information, based on actual tests, will help to produce a product of greater potency, especially in the Medicinal Herbs. Experiments involving tests and assays are costly but necessary to develop these crops properly. Much remains to be done by scientific research in the selection of better strains, production of choice seed and the establishment of preferred types. Work along these lines may prove of great benefit to the whole herb industry, which we hope has come to stay, in America.

THE COTTAGE GARDEN HERB INDUSTRY
SHERMAN K. and VERA B. HARDY

THE Cottage Garden Industry is generally understood to mean a self-contained unit where one or two individuals grow, harvest, dry and merchandise herbs for the retail trade, using a dozen or more of the important herbs for culinary preparations, herbal vinegars, pot pourris, sweet-bags, teas, lotions, hair washes and other specialized products. It differs from large scale commercial enterprises which place the emphasis on one or two herbs grown as a major crop for the wholesale trade.

With the upswing of interest in herbs, many requests for information have been sent to the Herb Society by people interested in making a profit from a small planting of herbs. It has been found that planting one herb crop designed for the wholesale market cannot be recommended as a profitable venture to the beginner, unacquainted with the culture of that particular herb and the standards required by the wholesale trade.

The small acreage does, however, lend itself to the Cottage Industry provided one does not expect to realize large profits immediately. The actual growing of most of the common herbs is not difficult; but growing the plant is by no means the major part of a successful Cottage Industry nor any guarantee that your particular herbal product will be acceptable to the public.

GROWING—Herb growing as a whole is a highly specialized field. The correct soil balance, time of harvest, drying method and final preparation all have their influence on the quality of the product offered. You can read all the text books there are on the subject and follow their rules to the letter and still end up with an inferior product. The only sound way to begin a Cottage Industry is to make a small start.

Over-fertilization with nitrogen is not desirable. Phosphate

The Cottage Herb Garden at Berkshire Garden Center, Berkshire, Mass.

and potash apparently have a beneficial reaction. Weeding and cultivation are always beneficial as a means of conserving moisture and driving the roots down, particularly in light soils. Mulching the plants after they are well established and shortly before cutting will alleviate the difficulty of dirty leaf.

HARVESTING—The time of harvest will vary with the individual herb and many theories have been advanced on this point without the substantiation of proof. A fair rule to follow is to consider the herb at its fullest potency just prior to or during bloom. Judging the correct cutting time will come from association with the herbs, although we hope to have more definite data on this point in the near future. The only way that a Cottage Garden on an intensive scale can be made to yield a profitable crop is by repeated cutting of the same plants, shearing being confined to the upper part of the plant so as to allow for recropping within two or three weeks.

DRYING—The method of curing or drying herbs is another controversial point and one on which we cannot generalize with any hope of accuracy, the underlying reason being the difference in the chemical elements of the essential oils in various herbs. In the light of present knowledge it is apparently true that drying in a semi-dark, dry, well aired room will preserve the color, aroma and flavor of the finished product. After drying, the leaf should be stored in a closed container, preferably not air tight, otherwise condensation and mould may set in. A lot of work has yet to be done on this matter of drying temperatures and the rapidity with which drying should take place.

PREPARATION—In preparing the dried herb for use one faces a different problem with each individual herb if its maximum value is to be preserved. Basil, thyme, angelica, mints work up readily and unusable stem can easily be screened out. Savory, marjoram, parsley and chervil are apt to be unmanageable if not bone dry. Sage on the other hand, with its tend-

Example of A Cottage Herb Garden at The Little House, Annisquam, Mass.

ency to dustiness, works better if a little on the leathery side. Herbal vinegars are at their best when fresh, as too long standing evidently releases chemical constituents that destroy the original ethereal quality.

MERCHANDISING—The properly managed Cottage Industry can be the most powerful means of reintroducing the use of herbs to the general public. To some merchandisers, a pretty package seems to be the one thing needful in a successful business. Unquestionably eye appeal is a powerful selling factor but if the merchandise within the pretty package falls short of the desirable qualifications of color, aroma and flavor, nothing will create more resentment in the public mind. You may expect permanence and expansion in giving the public an attractive package only if you give them something inside that will make them come back for more.

The green herb market holds distinct possibilities, but it has not yet taken hold in New England to the extent that it has along the Central Atlantic seaboard where the public apparently appreciates the value of tasty food. If more people understood what a delicacy they are missing by not using the green herb when it is at the height of its value, the green herb outlet would be enormous. Unquestionably missionary work is needed here and it will be up to a few courageous growers to work up this business by educating the consumer.

BASIC HERBS—Study the characteristics and reactions of your plants to the particular soil type you may have. Only by actually working with the herbs can you hope to get that sense of feel which recognizes the idiosyncracies and variations caused by changes of soil, weather and handling. The eventual goal of the conscientious herb grower is to produce desirable flavor and aroma in the product. Soil requirements vary with the individual herb, but a general qualification shows us that a good average garden soil, preferably on the light side, is suitable for thyme, parsley, basil, savory, marjoram, sage, tarragon, dill. A heavier soil type is preferable for angelica, lovage, mints, fennel, chives, chervil. This does not mean that you will get the maximum of leaf-yield from these soil types; maximum yield is not always indicative of most potent qualities.

The following list of herbs gives a general idea of a foundation to work from, in establishing a Cottage Herb Industry. The number of plants of each variety gives a fair balance in their proportion to each other, and their uses for marketing are indicated.

Herb	No. of plants	Dried	Vinegars	Savory Seeds	Green Herbs
Angelica	20	*		*	*
Basil	300	*	*		*
Burnet	100		*		*
Caraway	100			*	*
Catnip	200	*			*
Chervil	200	*			
Chives	150				*
Coriander	200			*	
Dill	200		*	*	*
Fennel	200		*		*
Lovage	25	*		*	*
Marjoram	150	*	*		*
Mints					
Lamb mint	50	*	*		*
Peppermint	50	*			
Spearmint	100	*	*		*
Parsley	200	*			*
Sage	50	*			*
Savory					
Summer	300	*	*		*
Winter	200	*			*
Sorrel, French	50				*
Tarragon	50	*	*		*
Thyme	500	*	*		*

Aromatics: — Lemon verbena, Rose geranium, Lavender, Rosemary, Marjoram.

"TWELVE BASKETS FULL"
FRANCES R. WILLIAMS

I WANTED an herb garden. My open porch was my sunniest place, in shadow only during the late afternoon hours. The porch is about nine feet square, having the house and a chimney on the west side, a screened porch on the north and low railings on the east and south.

I procured twelve low bushel baskets such as are used for vegetables, and four cases in which eggs are packed. I laid some discarded blinds on the porch floor, as if they were flower beds, and on these I arranged the baskets and egg cases.

Three baskets were set against the chimney, and opposite!

Mrs. Williams's Porch Herb Garden

them on the east side against the railing were three more baskets. A seat was put against the railing along the south side, and at each end of it was a square made of two egg cases. This seat faced a central panel of six baskets with a little path surrounding it.

Each basket and box was filled to within four inches of the top with half-rotted compost from my pile of garden refuse; over this base was put three inches of soil. I started to work out the area of each basket in square inches to find how much fertilizer would be needed, but found it was easier to fertilize a spot in my garden, dig in the fertilizer, and take soil from that. Thus on 50 square feet in the garden I added 2 pounds of 5-8-7, three cubic feet of sifted compost and 5 pounds of rock limestone to make up the soil for my herbs.

Summer savory seed was planted in the egg cases at the corner of the railings. The seedlings were thinned to six inches, leaving about 24 plants in the two boxes. In the pair of egg cases at the other end of the seat about a dozen sweet basil seedlings were planted, although they were rather crowded. Dill seed, planted in a basket beside the east railing, grew thick enough so that there were seedlings to be eaten and other plants left, about six inches apart, to grow for seed. Five lettuce-leaved basil seedlings were set out in another basket.

In each basket against the chimney was placed one tomato plant. They were the small-fruited varieties, red cherry, red and yellow pear and yellow plum. They each needed a couple of stakes and fell pleasantly over the edges of their baskets.

Three plants of narrow-leaved French thyme went into each basket just in front of the seat, in the central panel. Five sweet marjoram seedlings were put in each of the other bushel baskets. Two baskets had early spring marjoram seedlings that cut to yield a generous amount for drying, and their second growth in August looked the same height as the later seedlings in the other baskets.

The savory was harvested and pulled up when just about to blossom, and the dill when the seed was ripe. The thyme and marjoram in two baskets were sheared down when about to bloom and the plants left for further growth. Cuttings of basil were made all summer. Basil, sweet marjoram and thyme yielded enough for a crop to dry and then continued to grow until frost for use in green salads.

Bushel baskets and egg cases have such depth that they hold moisture a long time and so do not have to be watered every day. It was fun to weed a garden of that size, and the yield was most satisfactory.

AN IMPORTANT ADDITION TO AMERICANA

AN early 17th century Encyclopedia of the New World, discovered among the Vatican Library's manuscripts by Dr. Charles Upson Clark and translated by him, has just been published by the Smithsonian Institution, three centuries after the death of its author, Fray Antonio Vazquez de Espinosa. The existence of this massive work was known from references in contemporary writings, but it had been considered lost until Dr. Clark's discovery. This is the book referred to in a letter from Dr. Clark quoted among the Notes in the Herbarist for 1941, No. 7. It has taken him three years to prepare the work for publication. Our illustration, kindly supplied by the Smithsonian Institution, shows the first page of the book in print. Before his death de Espinosa had started with the printing of his book, in 1630, but only a hundred pages were in proof when he died.

Espinosa was a Spaniard, a native of Andalusia and a Carmelite friar. Most of what he describes he saw himself during half a lifetime spent in travelling over South and Central America. His geography was sometimes badly out of drawing, since he was a man of his times, writing soon after 1600. But he has given us one of the earliest descriptions of territory within the present bounds of the United States, New Mexico and possibly Kansas and Nebraska. He visited Mexico City and St. Augustine, Florida.

He makes no claim to be a historian; his interest was chiefly in ecclesiastical administration, and he made a careful survey of the church affairs in the dioceses he visited; but everything interested him, and he had an almost photographic eye. He collected scientific and practical facts; with his keen observation and curiosity he watched the Indians and their life, and noticed the flowers, trees, birds, beasts, scenery, and described them accurately. There is nothing here of the myths and fairy tales with which many early travellers padded their works. On a

Fol. 1

PRIMERA
PARTE DEL COMPENDIO Y DESCRIPCION DE LAS INDIAS OCIDENTALES.

LIBRO PRIMERO,

DEL ORIGEN Y DECENDENCIA DE LOS Indios: de que generaciones procedieron: quando y por donde passaron à poblar las Indias: muchos de sus ritos y costumbres, con otras calidades dignas de ser aduertidas: la nauegacion que hazen los Galeones y Flotas a ellas, y por donde bueluen à España.

CAPITVLO PRIMERO.

De la nauegacion que hazen a las Indias, y la buelta para España.

LOS galeones, flotas y demas nauios que nauegan à las Indias de la Nueua-España, Tierra-firme, y demas partes dellas, salen de Sanlucar de Barrameda, ò de Cadiz, que estan en 37.grados de altura de la Equinocial, desde donde salen, doblan la isla de Saluedina, que està media legua de Sanlucar al Sueste; en Verano se gouierna al Sudueste, y en Inuierno al Sudueste quarta al Sur hasta el Cabo de Cantin, que està en 32.grados, porque en la costa de Berberia se hallan brizas, desde dōde gouiernan al Sudueste quarta al Oeste, hasta la punta de Naga en la isla de Tenerife de las Canarias, que està en 28.grados.2 50.leguas de España, segun cuenta de Marineros, por donde ordinario passan a vista de las dichas islas: desde ellas nauegà por el golfo grande al Oessudueste hasta 20. grados; y desde aquel parage se gouierna al Oeste quarta al Sudueste hasta 15. grados y medio, desde donde nauegando al Oeste se dà en la isla Deseada, y si nauegaren por 15.en Marigalante, que seran mas de 750.leguas de las Canarias, y de España 1 ļj. en estas islas de Guadalupe, donde los galeones y flotas hazen agua, y toman algun refresco de gallinas, pescado, y frutas de la tierra que traen los Indios Gētiles de aquellas islas por rescate de hachas, cuchillos y otras cosas.

A   Aura

AN IMPORTANT ADDITION TO AMERICANA

First printed page of the Compendium and Description of the West Indies, by Antonio Vazquez De Espinosa.

Courtesy of the Smithsonian Institution, Washington, D. C.

river journey to Bogota he notes growing along the banks "many valuable trees from which are derived aromatic extracts," such as turpentine, balsam, benzoin, storax. He tasted of strange fruits, kernels, seeds, nuts, at no small risk to himself, it would seem. He pauses to notice that "sloths.... take a long time to raise their foot and make a step forward, making a great enterprise out of it."

Medicinal plants must have been a hobby of his and he contrasts what he saw with varieties he knew in Spain. References to herbs and their uses by the Indians of Central and South America abound, and we have the earliest known references to their use of quinine. He says: "From the quinaquina tree (cinchona) they get a liver-colored resin which is very fragrant and healing; with its vapor chills and head colds disappear; and with this resin mixed with oil they cure wounds and sores, and the oil which is pressed out from its seeds has the same virtue and is more efficacious. The quinaquina is a very handsome tree, and its wood is very fragrant and tough; the color of its wood is white with tawny streaks." He describes drug plants used in the treatment of chills, fever, poisoning, kidney and stomach ailments and many more; and he lists "Spanish Medicinal plants" such as rosemary, fennel, marjoram, rue, coriander, camomile, vervain, borage and countless other herbs, "the virtues of most of which are well known." He also observes "a vine which climbs like ivy and bears very fragrant and medicinally beneficial pods which they put in chocolate," namely vanilla.

The great compendium of facts which de Espinosa got together will be invaluable to anthropologist and historian and botanist alike. His present translator speaks of this "honest and earnest old Carmelite" with respect and affection, and after three years spent on this work calls him "one of the noblest and ablest of those scores of thousands who carried Spanish civilization and ideals to the New World."

FROM MAINE AND ALL ALONGSHORE
IRISH MOSS

FOR many generations, Irish sea moss (Chondrus crispus) has led a blameless life in the invalid's dietary along with colt'sfoot jelly and rennet. It has now been glamorized, and assumes a new importance as chemical research gives it modern uses.

The shores of the Atlantic Ocean from Norway to Gibraltar, the coasts of Ireland, and particularly the submerged rocks off the coast of Maine and Massachusetts have furnished the supply of this mucilaginous seaweed for medicinal and chemical uses and as a vehicle for various skin lotions and jellies, and it is well known to New England housewives as a simple dessert—the "blanc mange" of our childhood. The constituents of this curly clinger to our rocks, compounds of sodium, magnesium, potassium, calcium, chlorine, iodine, bromine, as well as its proteins, have now given it a new lease of life and usefulness; and since the supplies from France, Ireland and Norway have been curtailed by the loss of the freedom of the seas, gatherers along the New England coast have been stimulated to new activity in spite of the strict patrol. With the greater demand and higher prices, better methods of collecting are being developed and fishermen are taking advantage of this source of revenue.

The collectors go out in a fleet of dories, towed by a motor boat, and scrape the algae from the rocks at low tide with long-handled rakes. The collecting period is from May to September. The moss is first dried on the level sand, then placed on eight-foot elevated trays of small mesh wire. These trays are spread in the sun and watered daily with salt water by means of a donkey-engine and a long hose, until the moss is thoroughly bleached. It has been proven that salt water washing improves the product although some collectors still use fresh water. After being thoroughly washed the trays of moss remain in the sun for five days; in the case of heavy fog or rain, the trays are hastily stacked and covered with a tarpaulin. Five pounds of the wet moss reduce to one pound of dry product; the price naturally fluctuates with the supply and the quality.

"The Kitchen Directory and American Housewife," New York, 1859, gives the following among its recipes for Cookery for the sick:

"Steep Irish moss in cold water a few minutes, to extract the bitter taste, then drain off the water, and to half an ounce of moss put a quart of fresh water, and a stick of cinnamon. Boil it till of a thick jelly, strain and season to the taste with white sugar and wine, when it can be taken. Lemon-juice may be substituted for the wine, if it is not to be kept long. This is very nourishing, and highly recommended for consumptive complaints."

A present-day correspondent has little to add or change in this method, for she writes from the North Shore of Massachusetts: "My recipe for Irish Moss Blanc Mange was a quart of milk in the double boiler with a small handful (three or four pieces) of the moss. Cook until it gives a sort of jelly test and feels like boiled custard; add a teaspoon of salt and strain it into a mould like gelatine. Serve with cream and sugar and nutmeg. Gathering the moss was a summer task; it was washed in many waters to free it from sand, and bleached. It was a standard Christmas present for children to give grandmothers, put up neatly in bags or boxes of the children's own manufacture. Then there was a clear lemon concoction made with water and sea moss and flavored with lemon juice, for a cough."

Still another contribution comes from Rye Beach, New Hampshire, concerning "the humble Irish Moss, but not so humble now, and actually coming up in the world. It is being gathered again at Rye Harbor and we see it spread out to dry and bleach ....I continue to gather our own supply when it is washed up on our beach; I wash it in clear water and put it on a cloth in the sun on the lawn.... Our way of making the Blanc Mange is to put a small handful—two or three sprigs—of the moss, which has been rinsed in water, into 1 quart of milk and cook it 20 minutes in a double boiler; then strain through cheesecloth into a mould. That is all, no sweetening, no seasoning. Serve with cream and sugar. In these rationed days, here is a merit of this gentle dish: if you are fortunate enough to have jam or marmalade, it needs no sugar, the jam will sweeten it enough. It takes a little experimenting, for a cook is inclined to use too little, when it flops, or too much, when it is too stiff. The cheesecloth is necessary and no particles should be pressed through. People like it after they get over the idea that they are eating seaweed."

Flowers among the Ruins.—A surprising feature of bomb-blitzed London is the numerous wild-flowers which have sprung up from the brick dust and rubble in the heart of the city. The London Illustrated News for Sept. 19, 1942 gives pictures of hop-clover, golden rod, groundsel, willow-herb and ragwort in full flower with bees hovering about them, within a stone's throw of Holburn and Fleet Street. Conjectures arise as to whether seeds hidden for a hundred years beneath masonry and paving have at last germinated, or whether they have been blown there from a long distance by the great air disturbances caused by bombing.

EXPERIMENTS BY NEW ENGLAND MEMBERS

A REPORT ON BELLADONNA

BELLADONNA (atropa belladonna) was grown in Massachusetts in an experimental plot for two successive years, 1941 and 1942, not to prove or disprove that it was something to be commercially cultivated, but for seed. English growers have stated that experiments made in the culture of belladonna show that variations in climatic conditions affect its yield of alkaloids to a greater extent than any other environmental alterations.

The two summers were complete contrasts in weather: 1941 was hot and dry, 1942 was cool and moist. The plants were grown both years in the same soil and had the same cultivation. Seed was planted in the greenhouse February 15th and the first seeds sprouted 60 days later. While these first seedlings were developing, germination continued in the seed-pan, even after some seedlings were ready to be transplanted to flats. This uneven germination gave three sizes of plants; the third set of seedlings, which were the last to germinate, were weak plants and developed very slowly, while the first, which were set in the open in May, grew into strong, well-branched and healthy specimens. Constant spraying with rotenone was necessary to keep down the small beetles. The plants were in full bloom by September 1st, and gave a good crop of ripened seed. A heavy frost on September 1st did not affect the leafage, but for additional safety the crop was cut and dried.

The plants which were left in the ground with earth mounded up about them were completely winter-killed, while other plants which were put in cold frames unfortunately furnished an apparently nourishing winter diet for rabbits and rodents. Other plants from the same lots which were transplanted to other localities survived the winter and blossomed luxuriantly; some farther south in Little Compton, Rhode Island, were in an exposed position and uncovered, while plants in Saugus, Massachusetts were carefully protected by straw.

Cuttings from the plant root quickly, and on account of the slow germination of seed this would seem to be a more feasible method of increasing the stock.

DIGITALIS PURPUREA

The seed for an experiment with Digitalis was a selected seed from a medicinal garden. The seedlings, started in a greenhouse, were very strong plants, and this may account for the small percentage of winter-killing. After germination the seed-pans were transferred to a cool greenhouse, and very early in the spring to the cold-frame. This treatment was undoubtedly responsible for the lusty plants which developed under the most diverse conditions. The object of this experiment being to secure data as to growing in different localities and to select seed, very little of the leaf was dried to determine the potency. The result of the assay of dried leaf taken from different plots in the vicinity of Boston gave a high test, and as the leaf was selected from plants of most vigorous growth, these plants were marked after the test showing their excellence and seed from them was saved and marked.

The percentage of winter-killing varied. In northern New Hampshire, in spite of careful covering, 80% were lost. In the vicinity of Boston, 100% in one group and 50% in another were lost; in the latter case the planting was in a row and just one half died, though under the same conditions of exposure. All that was planted in wooded areas similar to that prevailing in the northwest where it grows wild, grew but did not flower, although heavy flower stalks developed, some eight and ten feet tall. The plants all came true to type and an average of one digitalis purpurea var. monstrosa would be found in each planting.

RAMIE

The experiment in growing Ramie (Boehmeria Nivea) as far north as Massachusetts has produced a strong, sturdy plant growing to a height of five to six feet. The leaves are opposite, coarsely toothed, with under surfaces white. Flowers are in axillary panicles, with staminate flowers in the lower part of the inflorescence. The seeds were very small and after three trials germinated in forty days; in the third trial the seed was sown in a mixture of rotted leaf mould and sand, very finely sifted. Transplanted into seed flats, they developed into sturdy plants ready to transplant into the open in May after danger of frost was over. The season was cool with plenty of moisture, and insects were not a problem.

This member of the nettle family is the most important textile plant in China and is found growing wild as well as cultivated, in all the warm parts of the Middle Kingdom. In Hupeh the wild plant is called Ch'uma, and the cultivated Hsien-Ma. Travellers in Szechuan are constantly impressed by the small patches of this "China grass" which are to be seen growing around nearly every peasant's home. The fibre used in weaving the sandals commonly worn by the Chinese is made of this grass which is unusually tough and strong. Its excellent durable bast fibers are also used for strong thread and upholstery fabrics. Ramie is being cultivated experimentally in the western United States, and if it can be successfully grown will greatly relieve the shortage in fiber plants caused by the war.

ENGLAND'S KITCHEN FRONT

AS these words are being written, America is just beginning to feel the first serious shortages, and trial schemes for our first national ration-books are being drawn up. It may be of interest to see how the problem of feeding a nation in war time has been successfully worked out by our Allies. A program like theirs means work; not a few minutes now and then, but a woman's whole-time attention; for we must accustom ourselves to the fact that we can no longer count on buying food wholly or partially prepared for the table.

Very early in the war, the question of Britain's national health, the task of feeding its fighting men, its women warworkers doing man's labor, and its children, assumed the most urgent importance. There must have been frightening moments as they saw the shrinkage of food supplies and thought of the small size of their island and the increasing difficulty of getting foodstuffs from outside. It became evident that here was a problem calling for a plan on a national scale. If everyone had not risen to the emergency unanimously and with determination, there might have been a catastrophe. So English housewives went into action, and their reward has been that the public health has been maintained, everyone has had enough to eat, share and share alike, and serious epidemics have been avoided in spite of crowded and abnormal living conditions. The "Kitchen Front" is helping to win the war.

The British Ministry of Food issued a series of Food Facts in the newspapers and weeklies with purchasing tips and even recipes. A fair and scientifically balanced rationing system based on a family's needs was worked out, and regulations were enforced in public restaurants. The reclaiming of waste land and the harvesting of wild material were urged. Above all, people began a serious study of the art of cooking, of making the limited and rather dull staples interesting and palatable. A "national loaf" of light brown bread of 85 per cent wheatmeal was set up as a standard and is the only bread obtainable. Country people and school children garner every blade and leaf, nut and berry that is edible; to combat the shortage in medicinal herbs too, depots were established in many parts of the country and between 300 and 400 tons of herbs were collected by the children last summer. Dandelion, peppermint, coltsfoot, sage, thyme, motherwort, fennel, rue and horehound are a few of the plants the children have learned to recognize and bring in. Vitamins are studied and a balanced diet worked out. Onions grow where tulips blossomed in the flower beds, and runner beans instead of roses, and herbs are in demand not only to take the place of formerly imported condiments and seasonings, but as a protective food. And now England is producing within its island limits two-thirds of all the food it needs.

We are quoting by kind permission of the British Broadcasting Corporation, excerpts from an article by Anne Scott-James in "London Calling," entitled "What We Are Eating in England Today."

"The war has stirred up a revolution in English cooking; none too soon, I expect you'll say. We used to be notorious as the worst cooks in the world, but I honestly think we are quite good cooks now. We have learnt, after centuries of solid meat-eating, the Continental art of making vegetable dishes. We have adopted, after centuries of throwing spare food down the drain, the French trick of keeping a stockpot and making good, cheap soups. We have revived the old-fashioned arts of preserving fruit and vegetables, so that we have our summer surplus in the winter in the form of jams, pickles, dried and bottled fruit and vegetables. We've looked out French recipe books and learnt to make salads and sauces.... Today we can nearly all ask you to supper and make you happy on good vegetables, rice, one egg, a tomato or two, and odds and ends of meat or bacon. The less you have to cook with the better you cook, it seems.

"Then householders all over the country are supplementing the food they buy in the shops with home-grown foods. Every person with so much as a pocket handkerchief of garden has packed it with vegetables, not only in the country but in London, too. I have some friends in London with no garden at all who grow tomatoes on their balcony, herbs and salads in pots in their kitchen, and runner beans up strings in their square inch of paved back yard. People with large gardens have turned over lawns, tennis courts, flower beds to vegetables. People with small gardens have made themselves entirely self-supporting in vegetables and fruit. People with no gardens at all have taken up allotments in the neighborhood. Even in industrial cities, rabbits and hens, pigs and bees are being kept most successfully for food.

"Have you ever eaten potato pastry? I hadn't before the war. But another of the things our research cooks have taught us is how versatile vegetables are. Pastry made with mashed potato instead of flour tastes exactly like ordinary pastry. I won't say that carrot marmalade is as good as orange marmalade, but it's quite a pleasant breakfast substitute. Wild foods that used to rot in the woods are now gathered for cooking. Wild hip-berries have been found to contain more vitamin C than oranges and are made into juice for babies. Villagers go collecting hazel nuts now that we have no imported almonds. Crab apples go into jelly. Country people now find a use for stinging-nettles, which grow in profusion in the English countryside. They even go so far as to organize stinging-nettle parties, when the whole village turns out for a hard—and often painful—day's work. Iced herb drinks, such as lime (linden) tea, are served in summer instead of fruit juices. And we dig in Victorian recipe books for formulas for country wines. Elderberry, parsnip, and dandelion wine are made now in many country houses where they would have been thought an eccentricity before....

"Everyone in Britain now takes a passionate interest in food. You hear Press lords talking about it in the Savoy Grill; workmen discussing it in canteens; maiden ladies exchanging recipes at vicarage work-parties.... I think that this goes to show, not that we're greedy, not that we're hungry, but that we are all subconsciously aware how much food means to us, an island nation, in this fight."

The HERBARIST *for* 1943
A Limited Edition
Written and Published by
THE HERB SOCIETY *of* AMERICA
PRICE $1.00

A few copies of previous years are still available at $1.00 each

Other publications of the Herb Society of America

PLACE OF THE DRIED HERB IN INDUSTRY. (1937).	.05
BELLADONNA. Reprint from the Herbarist. (1941)	.25
LIST OF GARDENS AND HERBARIA DEVOTED TO MEDICINAL AND OTHER HERBS. Second Edition, (1941).	.15
RECORDS OF A GROUP OF SAGE GROWERS. (1942).	.25
FERTILIZER TESTS ON HERBS. (1942).	.05
AN HERB DRIER FOR DIGITALIS, J. A. Patch. Reprint from Annual Report. (1942).	.15
THE HOME GROWING OF TWELVE CONDIMENT HERBS. Second Edition. (1942).	.25
THE USE AND METHODS OF MAKING AN HERBARIUM. (1942).	.25
THE COTTAGE HERB INDUSTRY. Reprint from Herbarist. (1943).	.15
SAGE BULLETIN NO. 3, INCLUDING NEW FERTILIZER TESTS. (1943).	.25

Free Publications:
SOME SOURCES OF HERB SEEDS, PLANTS, AND DRIED PRODUCTS, Information Sheet No. 5. (1942).
A SUGGESTED READING LIST OF HERBS, Information Sheet No. 6. (1943).

Address
THE HERB SOCIETY *of* AMERICA
HORTICULTURAL HALL
300 Massachusetts Avenue　　　　　　Boston, Massachusetts

FIELD NOTES

Paprika Experiment.—Yugoslavia has been the main source of paprika, so familiar in all American kitchens. When the imported supply fell off, one man, a Hungarian by birth named Denese, now an American citizen, succeeded in obtaining a small package of dried paprika pods. The seed was sown at the Department of Agriculture's proving grounds at Beltsville, and from this small beginning a new crop is growing in St. Landry Parish, Louisiana, where soil conditions are suited to it. Farmers there were poor and badly needed a new crop, and had large families to provide the labor. A mill has been established to dry, clean and grind the red powder, and a distinctly American paprika is being produced which is said to be even better than the European variety.

Kapok Substitute.—Milkweed floss proves to be warmer and lighter than wool, and buoyant enough to be of great value for flying suits and navy life jackets. Minute air cells running through its fiber are sealed in by the waxy substance which can be felt in handling it, and a suit lined with the floss will keep a man afloat for 100 hours. In northwestern Michigan a corporation has been formed, and people are actually at work on a large scale gathering milkweed pods from wild plants; commercial production for next year is being encouraged. After a de-waxing process, the floss can also be used for bandages, and in fact the whole milkweed plant bids fair to win some fame in the war.

Trefoil for Soil.—In New Hampshire a new legume is being grown as a soil modifier which may prove extremely useful in reclaiming the acid soil of run-out hayfields and pastures. It is bird'sfoot trefoil, which seems better adapted to poor soils than clover. It is slow to start, requiring 2 to 3 years to get well established, but will last for years, and cattle like it as hay. It should be grown as a hay crop the first year and cut, before animals are allowed to graze it.

Fragrance.—Not many reference books make entertaining reading; but a book which is a pleasant mixture of romantic tales of "far Cathay" and the Seven Seas, combined with facts illustrated with photographs and useful drawings, is "Perfumes and Spices," by A. Hyatt Verrill (Boston, L. C. Page & Co.). In reading of the origin and history of spices, flavor plants and perfumes we range over the world and find that we have added to our herbal knowledge as well. The chapter headings give an idea of such diverse subjects as how spices led to explorations and discoveries; the vanilla orchid; perfume insecticides; soapy plants; incense and sachets.

Save All Seeds.—A graphic reminder of what the scorched earth policy will mean comes in a plea for seeds of all kinds in a European review now being published in New York. Not only has the commercial production of seed been brought to a standstill in Europe, but the results of years of scientific production, records of tests and new strains and precious equipment have been deliberately "liquidated." Added to this, nature's own reproductive work has been stopped by the sterilization and neglect of the soil on a vast scale. The countries which formerly produced a large part of the world's seed supply will be obliged to import great quantities for years to come, first of all for food. Everything men need and consume derives from this source and the need will take on such dimensions that the planning for post war supplies cannot begin too soon. Raising seed for our own uses at least relieves the pressure upon the public supply.

OUR CONTRIBUTORS
Editor
MARTHA GENUNG STEARNS

CAROLINE WEIR ELY contributes another drawing in the series she has made for our frontispiece.

MRS. ARTHUR B. BAER is the Chairman of the St. Louis Unit, G.C.A., and her well-documented paper on Angelica is the result of much research into this herb's uses in commerce.

COLONEL EDGAR ERSKINE HUME, Medical Corps, U. S. Army, has been for several years the Director of Administration at the Medical Field Service School, Carlisle, Pa., and is the author of many books and papers on medical and historical subjects.

HELEN MORGENTHAU FOX needs no introduction to herbalists, since her book "Gardening with Herbs" is in the reference library of every gardener. In this article she gives us a preview of the subject of her forthcoming book, "Gardening for Good Eating," now in the press.

SHERMAN K. and VERA B. HARDY are enthusiastic herb-gardeners and are well qualified to write on their subject, operating a Cottage Garden in Lexington, Mass.

FRANCES R. WILLIAMS, Curator of the Society's herbarium, has made noteworthy experiments in methods of drying plants and flowers for herbaria, in addition to research in many other lines.

MISS MARY EARLE GOULD, who photographed a group of wooden utensils from her collection, is the author of a new book, "Early American Wooden Ware," a thorough study of this subject which has not been previously covered.

Rose-hips for Vitamins.—The war has introduced the value of Rose-hips to the English people, who are carefully harvesting both the hedge rose and garden varieties. These are said to be even more rich than oranges in Vitamin C, and have a pronounced effect on the health of the body's intercellular substance, the cartilage, gums and blood vessels. Good suggestions for simple ways of adding them to the diet come from the Scandinavian countries where they have long been used. The hips are allowed to grow to full size and ripeness; the part to be used is the layer of firm flesh just inside the bright skin, and the skin and seeds are discarded. Being so small, they are used with other fruits in jam and jelly, and cooked with honey and pudding sauces. The flavor when cooked down alone is very pleasant and gentle, and not quite like any other fruit.

Third Printing

Herbs

How to Grow Them and How to Use Them

By HELEN NOYES WEBSTER

Complete — Practical — Low Priced

Here you will find famous plans of herb gardens: lists for planting period gardens and for herb families; the herbs to use in modern gardens; valuable information about the use of herbs; and of course complete cultural information. Written by one of the country's leading authorities, it will make it easy to have an herb garden that will be a delight to you and the envy of your friends.

198 pages...36 illustrations, Octavo only, $1.25. Postpaid in U. S.

Make checks payable to

HORTICULTURE, Horticultural Hall, Boston, Mass.

THE HERB SOCIETY OF AMERICA
OFFICERS AND DIRECTORS
1942 - 1943

OFFICERS

President-at-Large	Dr. E. D. Merrill
President	Mrs. John H. Cunningham
Vice-president	Mrs. A. C. Burrage Jr.
2nd Vice-president	Mrs. Foster Stearns
Secretary	Mrs. Laurence A. Brown
Treasurer	Miss Margaret Norton

STANDING COMMITTEES

Botanical Research and Bibliography	Mrs. Hollis Webster
Curator of Herbarium and Publicity	Mrs. Frances R. Williams
Commercial Research and Publication Committee	Mrs. E. B. Cole
The Herbarist	Mrs. Foster Stearns, *Editor*

DIRECTORS

Mrs. Pierce Archer	Mrs. John Gibbon
Mrs. Arthur B. Baer	Mrs. Alfred Kay
Mrs. G. Page Ely	Mrs. E. L. Mitchell
Mrs. Robert Fife	Mrs. Alfred Stengel
Miss E. Van Brunt	Mrs. Spencer Thorpe
Mrs. Donald Durant	Mrs. H. H. Richards

Mr. and Mrs. Sherman K. Hardy

UNIT CHAIRMEN

Philadelphia:
  Mrs. John H. Gibbon, Lynfield Farm, Media, Penna.
New York:
  Miss Elizabeth Remson Van Brunt, Kitchawan, N. Y.
St. Louis:
  Mrs. Arthur B. Baer, 9425 Ladue Road, St. Louis Co., Mo.
California:
  Mrs. Spencer Thorpe, 339 South Kingsley Dr., Los Angeles, Cal.
New England:
  Mrs. John H. Cunningham, 53 Seaver Street, Brookline, Mass.
Western Reserve:
  Mrs. A. E. Boethelt, 5925 Corydon Rd., Clev. Hts., Ohio.
Portland, Oregon:
  Miss Arlie Seaman, 2755 S. W. Summit Drive, Portland, Ore.

The HERBARIST

*A Publication of
The Herb Society of America*

No. 10

For Use and for Delight

BOSTON, MASSACHUSETTS

1944

Newcomb & Gauss Co., Printers
Salem, Massachusetts

Copyright, 1944, by The Herb Society of America

C O N T E N T S

	PAGE
FRONTISPIECE: The Kitchen Garden at Mount Vernon	4
FOREWORD	5
HERBS AT MOUNT VERNON	7
THE NATIONAL GEOGRAPHIC SOCIETY INTEREST IN USEFUL PLANTS *Gilbert Grosvenor*	10
HERBS IN HIGH ALTITUDES	13
LOVAGE	14
NEW ORLEANS USES HERBS *Caroline D. Weiss*	17
THE AROMATIC LIFE *Martha Genung Stearns*	22
THE CIMARUTA	28
HOME MADE INKS *Catherine H. Sweeney*	29
THE INTER-AMERICAN QUININE PROGRAM	33
HERBS FOR CLEVELAND *Lucile M. Boethelt*	39
RECIPES WITH A DIFFERENCE	40
VEGETABLES PREPARED FOR PETS *Frances R. Williams*	43
SOME BOOKS OF THE PAST WITH HERBAL INTEREST	44
FIELD NOTES	47
TWO INSECT PESTS *Helen Noyes Webster*	49
OUR CONTRIBUTORS	52
THE COLLECTOR'S DREAM	54

The Kitchen Garden at Mount Vernon

FOREWORD

AS we review the attempts of the Society during the last three years to help growers to meet the shortage of herbs, a rather new picture is forming as to our responsibility for the future.

In the beginning there was little or no technical information about the growing of herbs commercially. To grow by the ton was quite a different problem from growing a few pounds; there was no guide as to yield or cost of growing per acre, and added to this dearth of knowledge there was little or no stock or seeds.

With these handicaps, some growers in 1941 were induced to undertake the planting of sage and digitalis either from patriotic motives or with the hope of adding a minor crop to their farm income. The year of 1941 was a year of drought, which piled up the handicaps, with the result that the first crop was limited in quantity and not up to standard in color or ash content. But it was sold, and the growers gained some valuable experience as a return for their expenditure of time and capital.

The 1942 season, starting with stock and experience, gave the growers a larger opportunity, and they harvested a crop of better quality, which sold at a fair profit.

The year 1943 has a still different story. As some importations commenced to trickle in, there was increasing optimism in the trade that the cheaper imported herb would soon become available, with a consequent reluctance among the buyers to make contracts with American growers. As a result, many acres of sage and other herbs were ploughed up and planted to vegetables and valuable herb stock was lost, because the grower, faced by labor shortage and the pressure placed upon making his land grow more vegetables, and with no security that his herb crop could be sold, felt that he should no longer take the risks of so speculative a crop.

In this country the herb harvest will generally be from cultivated areas; that means that each herb's reaction to soil and fertilizer must be studied. Given this knowledge and with improved varieties, America can produce a superior product, but not in competition in price and quality with the cheaper labor and wild product across the seas. To this end the Herb Society has done sound preliminary work*, and we hope that some farm people will continue to stay in the growing and help to re-establish this old industry on a basis of quality and flavor, and that the tide will turn in their favor; though it looks at the end of this 1943 year as if the hard-won experience and moderate success of these three years might slip away from our growers at the end of the war. Are we too altruistic in not starting a drive for American products, with the slogan: "Ask for all American herbs"?

Meanwhile the Society will continue to carry on and to publish its experimental work. It is our opinion, further, that the emphasis of the Society should be placed on Cottage Gardens, where herbs are grown for quality and skilful blending. With such a trademark the grower should secure and hold his own clientele. Our work is already taking on educational importance, as the public comes to notice and inquire concerning the place of herbs in our domestic concerns.

A. P. C.

*See Bulletins I, II and III, 1941-2-3, on tabulated data of growing and fertilizer tests.

HERBS AT MOUNT VERNON

THE Mount Vernon Kitchen Garden was restored in 1936 in a manner true to the time of General Washington. The General had brought the garden to the present size and shape just one hundred and fifty years earlier and in his writings, frequently referred to it. At the time the restoration was undertaken, no trace remained of the original patterns of beds and paths.

In evolving the new design, the books which the General owned and used, and the work accounts which he kept, were carefully studied. In the books were found plans of gardens with precise directions for the laying out of the ground and for the culture of the plantings. From the General's writings came the names of most of the things which are grown.

All of the plants now to be seen in the garden were familiar to the eighteenth century gardener. The amounts of each which are planted are in proportion to the requirements of a household such as the General maintained. A supply of water is kept in the different parts of the garden in "Basons.... where it may be exposed to the open Air and Sun, that it may be soften'd thereby; for such water as is taken out of Wells, Etc. just as it is used, is by no Means proper for any Sort of Plants." *From the Description accompanying the plan of the gardens.*

Mr. Charles W. Wall, Superintendent, Mount Vernon Ladies' Association, writes:

"In the restoration of the old kitchen garden at Mount Vernon, herbs have been used quite extensively, principally as borders for the beds. We know that they were features of the typical kitchen garden of the period, and we feel certain that when Washington wrote to his manager, 'Tell the Gardener I shall expect everything that a Garden ought to produce, in the most ample manner,' his generalization included herbs. Our present

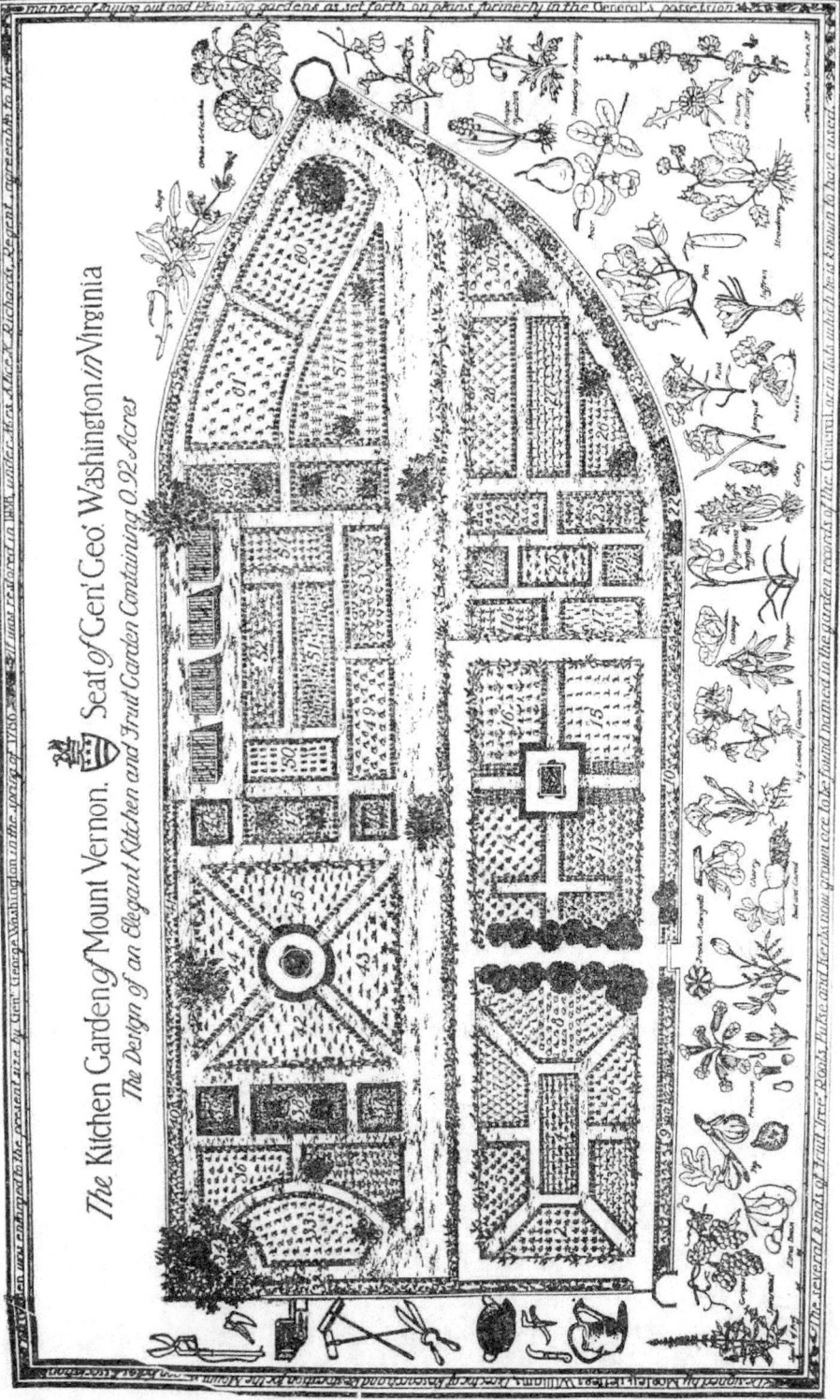

gardener is an enthusiast on the subject of herb culture and has considerable success with this activity as well as with curing and blending them for various uses."

The herbs which are listed in the typical planting plan of the Kitchen Garden are:

Sweet basil	Santolina	Mint
Horse radish	Chives	Mugwort
Sage	Rosemary	Sweet fennel
Nepeta	Winter savory	Rue
Thyme	Lavender	Parsley
Germander	Pennyroyal	Lemon balm
Sweet marjoram	Calendula	

The restoration of the gardens at Mount Vernon was done by Mr. Morley Williams, Director of Research and Restoration for the Mount Vernon Ladies' Association. In the preliminary plans for the kitchen garden he was assisted in the selection of the herbs by two members of the Herb Society of America, Mrs. Hollis Webster and Mrs. Samuel B. Kirkwood.

"Speak not—whisper not;
Here bloweth thyme and bergamot;
Softly on the evening hour,
Secret herbs their spices shower."
  From "Time Passes, and Other Poems,"
  by Walter de la Mare

THE NATIONAL GEOGRAPHIC SOCIETY'S INTEREST IN USEFUL PLANTS
By GILBERT GROSVENOR
Editor of the National Geographic Magazine

THE overwhelming importance of plant life in setting the stage for a livable world must be kept in mind in any comprehensive treatment of geography. Recognizing this, the National Geographic Society includes botanists in the personnel of many of the expeditions which it sends to remote parts of the world.

The Society has even dispatched complete expeditions primarily to search for certain plants; notably the party sent in 1937 to the mountainous region of northeast Kwangsi Province, in south China, to seek the source of the lo-han fruit. This fruit, highly prized in China for its medicinal qualities, had been bought and sold in dried form in Chinese markets for centuries, yet the plant producing it was unknown to science. The Society's expedition found the plant to be a vine cultivated and artificially pollinated by primitive, shy hill folk. Specimens of leaf, flower, and dried fruit, and photographs of the vine were brought to the United States and classified by Dr. Walter T. Swingle, botanist of the U. S. Department of Agriculture. The newly found plant was named by Dr. Swingle, "Momordica Grosvenori."

Expeditions of The Society, outstanding because of the wealth of botanical materials obtained, were led some years earlier by Joseph F. Rock into central and western China, and the eastern edge of Tibet. Dr. Rock brought back 60,000 sheets of herbarium specimens representing about 12,000 numbers. These are carefully preserved in the U. S. National Museum.

Dr. Rock brought also seeds and living plants. The seeds of 493 kinds of rhododendron which he introduced represented the richest addition to America's store of these ornamentals that has yet been made. Many of the beautiful new varieties of rhododendron are now growing luxuriantly in San Francisco's Golden Gate Park and in Kew Gardens, London. He brought also sets of rare gentians, primroses, and other Alpine plants.

Probably the most important economic contribution of these expeditions was the introduction of new blight-resistant chestnut trees at a time when the native American chestnut was on the way to complete extermination by blight. The immigrant chestnuts were planted at the U. S. Plant Introduction Garden at Glendale, Maryland, and have grown into sturdy trees. Improved strains have been bred from this material and later arrivals, and many young trees have been distributed. Last autumn on my farm I gathered two quarts of nuts from Rock's immigrants.

One of the world's most picturesque and ingenious types of agriculture was uncovered by an expedition to Peru sent by The Society in cooperation with Yale University. O. F. Cook, botanist of the expedition studied the remains of irrigated staircase farms of the ancient Peruvians — great tiers of terraces, held in place by walls of excellent masonry, that climbed steep valley slopes for 500 feet and more.

Here was the original home of the potato, and the expedition found dozens of species of the tuber still grown in the region. Investigations indicated that the staircase farmers, like their present day successors on the valley floors, cultivated corn, fruits, root crops, seed crops, pot herbs, condiments, medicinal and dye plants, and ornamentals.

The Society has shown its continuing interest in herbs and other plants by the publication of numerous articles and pictures in the National Geographic Magazine and in book form.

In The Geographic, the late Federick V. Coville, botanist of the U. S. Department of Agriculture, and for many years Chairman of the Committee on Research of the National Geographic Society, gave the first popular narrative of his fascinating discoveries by which he domesticated the blueberry and also greatly increased the size and quality of the fruit.

His researches proved that healthy, thrifty blueberries are dependent on the health of a microscopic fungus on its roots. Since the fungus can not grow well in fertile soil, neither can the plant. He found, on the other hand, that the berries grow with great vigor in acid soil, supposedly worthless for agriculture. As a result of his work blueberries can now be grown under cultivation. Varieties which he bred by many years of experiment and which are as large as Concord grapes are growing on blueberry plantations in the pine barrens of New Jersey and North Carolina.

Articles and colored illustrations on wild flowers and common plants of the countryside have been published over many years by The Society's Magazine. Among the many articles and groups of illustrations on these subjects that have appeared in the National Geographic Magazine are "Our State Flowers," "Exploring the Mysteries of Plant Life," "Familiar Grasses and Their Flowers," "Family Tree of the Flowers," "Flower Pageant of the Midwest," "Midsummer Wild Flowers," "Wild Flowers of the West," and a series on the wild flowers of California.

Few of the diverse chapters in the story of the building of America are more stimulating than those which deal with our plant immigrants. Brought with the greatest care across oceans and continents, they have contributed in a few years gardens and fields, orchards and forests of plants that Nature, in her ages of evolution, had never created in our land. Some of these plants have added hundreds of millions of dollars of value to the country's products. Through the years the Society's Magazine has told the story of the adventures and discoveries of the intrepid government plant explorers who have ransacked far-away valleys and mountains and deserts, seeking good things of the plant world to bring to our shores. Leaders in this little group have been David Fairchild, Frank N. Meyer, P. H. and J. H. Dorsett, Joseph F. Rock, Frederick Wulsin and Wilson Popenoe.

HERBS IN HIGH ALTITUDES

THE High Yemen, the mountain region inland from the southwestern coast of Arabia bordering on the Red Sea, is one of the loftiest in the world, running up to 10,500 feet; and perhaps it is not surprising that it still contains many unexplored areas. Hugh Scott, in his book "In the High Yemen," (London, John Murray, 1942) describes a visit to Ibb, "in some ways the most wonderful of all the cities of the Yemen. The impression left by it is of one of the very kernels of the East .... some 6,700 feet above sea-level, on a westward-projecting spur of Jebel Shemahe, which rises behind it to over 8,000 feet."

In the city of Ibb Mr. Scott talked with residents and officials, noting down his observations in vivid language, and here is a note of herbal interest:

"From the son, a bright and friendly little boy named Ahmed ibn Yahya, I at last got a chance to see the various herbs grown in pots (and too often in paraffin tins) on house roofs. I had many times gazed up at such roof-gardens from outside tall houses. Now this little Ahmed reeled off the Arabic names of rue, two kinds of basil, a sort of southernwood and other herbs. Sweet Basil (ocinum basilicum) was met with many times later in our journey; bunches of sprigs are stuck in men's turbans at marriage-ceremonies and other festivities; little beds of the plant were seen in corners of orchards near San 'a, and we were told that the fragrant herb is placed between clothes stored in chests."

LOVAGE

LOVAGE (*levisticum officinales*) is an old-timer among the herbs, which has been sadly neglected in the past generation or two. Too few people are aware of its virtues and it deserves to be revived as one of our familiar culinary herbs. It is distinguished by its strong celery flavor and aroma, and was used as a celery substitute by our forefathers, being easy to grow, and adaptable to almost any soil, though its favorite environment is a rather moist heavy soil with a good deal of shade. Here it will grow to a height of seven or eight feet and send up a flower stalk another foot. The umbellacious seed-head stands far above the main plant; if the seed is not to be used, the stalk can be cut out early and a greater growth of leaf induced; but its aromatic seeds attract birds, especially goldfinches, which should endear it to the garden lover. It is tall enough to make a handsome background plant in the border.

Lovage, or wild celery, appears in the list of household herbs in Walafrid Strabo's Little Garden, and it grew in the Herbularius or medicinal herb garden of the famous Abbey of St. Gall, which takes it back to the 8th century. In old New England the root used to be candied in sugar syrup in the same way as sweetflag root, as a candy and a breath purifier, and was called Smallage by our grandmothers. It was very largely grown for sale at the Shaker colonies. A lovage leaf will alleviate the pain from a bee-sting if crushed and rubbed on. The aromatic celery-like leaves are very good in salads, and there are few soups or stews in which an onion is considered essential, where a few lovage leaves would not be equally welcome.

The plant may be left in the clump indefinitely, after it is established in some damp corner near a pool or garden faucet; but a quicker method of increase than growing from seed is to divide

"Lovage"

From Woodville's "Medical Botany."—1832 Vol. I. Page 140.

the clumps every two or three years. The seed when maturing is subject to attack from carrot fly and aphids, if the birds don't get it.

Lovage is known to modern commerce as a source of oil for flavoring tobaccos and for perfumes, and the root in medicinal preparations. But one wonders why it has disappeared so generally from the herb patch where thyme, sage and parsley are still known and used.

"The Chinese make a trellis or "tepee" of tall poles and plant cucumbers around each pole. As the vines grow they are trained to climb up the trellis instead of spreading on the ground. The cucumbers hang down inside the "tepee." About four times as many cucumbers can be raised in a given area by this method since the vertical is used instead of the horizontal."

Paul Keene, in "The Decentralist."

NEW ORLEANS USES HERBS

By CAROLINE D. WEISS

CONNOISSEURS who have marvelled at the exquisite food served in New Orleans restaurants have always asked, "What is the secret of the New Orleans cuisine?" The question cannot be answered in a word. The fact is that many influences, historical, traditional, racial and even environmental, have contributed to its evolution.

New Orleans is unique among the cities of the United States in that it has lived under three flags: the French, the Spanish and the American. Upon this national foundation was grafted the Creole influence. The Creole was the native white group made up of people of either French or Spanish descent or a combination of the two. The educated Creoles were the first American group which developed artistic surroundings. New Orleans early in its history became noted for opera, drama, and the art of *"la joie de vivre."* Some of the amusements were even based on religious rites, such as the Mardi Gras, a last celebration before the solemn days of Lent. With such people it seems logical that eating should be more artistic and based on tradition than in other cities.

After the city of New Orleans was founded in 1718, the first influx of people were of the lower classes of France. Later a more aristocratic element arrived. The *"filles de cassette"* from good French families came to become the wives of these settlers. It has been said that these females swore to leave the colony if the food did not improve. In fact they themselves developed new standards of good cooking, based on Parisian customs and adapted to this country. At the time of the French Revolution, members of the French nobility came, and elegance of habit and manner of life began.

When Louis XV ceded New Orleans to Spain, there was marked Spanish influence in the architecture and in the piquant and peppery seasoning of some foods as well. However, 1801 saw the sale of Louisiana to France, and 1803 to the United States. French habits and manners went on and the Creoles, or natives, lived apart from the new American influx. The years have wrought slow changes.

With this historical background we can trace the traditions and influences that have created the rare New Orleans cuisine. It has for ancestry the frugal French customs, the Parisian elegance, a Spanish influence in some highly seasoned dishes, and the later ingenious and naive Negro adaptation of all these into food for practical Americans. Some small note must be taken of the Indian contribution. The Choctaws, a friendly tribe, gathered, dried and ground sassafras leaves which they used as a medicinal tea called *Filé*. They brought it, along with baskets, hides and other products to the French market. It was the Negro cook who had instinctive ideas about herbs and a genius for combining foods, who found that the *Filé* powder would thicken and flavor the Gumbo soup. The Negroes also gave us the beloved red beans and rice, and the Jambalaya.

The use of herbs in New Orleans cookery is neither new nor revived. It has always been. Once almost everyone grew tarragon, chervil, marjoram, rosemary, chives, basil, angelica, and had a French bay tree (laurus nobilis) in the garden. Now, the French market and some of the neighboring markets have fresh thyme and bayleaf as well as parsley, but the more subtle herbs that were once in every Creole garden must be purchased from the spice houses in the dried state, or omitted from the foods; not many of us have herb gardens.

Sunday in New Orleans has always been a great day for eating. I love to picture the scene we read of in old books. Sunday morning after church, the Creole ladies and gentlemen would go from the Cathedral to the near by French market to purchase food for the large dinner. They would have breakfast about eleven, the *grand dejeuner*, then go to the Matinee at the Opera House, and about six they would have dinner, with the elegant foods. But on week-days, and when the budget was strained, the foods introduced by the peasants were prepared. Typical of this is the *soup-en-famille* with the *bouilli* (beef brisket), or the Negro favorite, red beans and rice. These same simple dishes save our ration budget today.

Even in the modest restaurants the food is carefully seasoned. One does not see the salt and peppers shakers on each table, as is the American custom elsewhere. Some like food very highly seasoned, and for these there is served a bottle of pepper vinegar or tabasco sauce made from peppers grown in this section. Mark Twain, Thackaray, Irvin S. Cobb and others have turned fine phrases about New Orleans food, so I shall not wax literary, but will hasten on to the practical *"fait accompli."*

Now in the year 1944 we have rationing, and in New Orleans we don't mind. We can manage so well with meat of few points and fish of many kinds; our knowledge of cookery can make these taste as delicious as a rare roast of beef.

Before the student of Creole foods experiments with the seasoning and spices, there are two things she must learn. One is the correct preparation of rice, which must be the partner of the gumbo and the gravies. The other is how to make a *Roux*, the gravy that goes with almost every Creole dish.

Rice is cooked thus: Wash and pick the rice clean of any hulls or foreign matter. Rinse three times in cold water. Put a quart of water on the fire and let it boil vigorously, adding a teaspoonful of salt. Add a cupful or more of the well-washed rice while the water is boiling. The boiling water will toss the grains of rice and prevent them from clinging together. As soon as the grains commence to soften, do not touch or stir the rice again; let it continue to boil for 20 to 25 minutes, or until the grains begin to swell out and feel soft if pressed between the fingers. Pour off the water, put the rice in a colander and pour cold water over it, then let it steam over a pot of boiling water until dry. Boiled rice is served with chicken, turkey, crab or shrimp gumbo, peas, beans, meat balls, *grillades, daube,* with gravies of all kinds, and as the base for Jambalaya.

Jambalaya is a dish of rice to which is added oysters and chopped ham, or small cut up sausages. It is started by browning a chopped onion, two tablespoonsful of flour, one of butter or lard, and adding to this six tomatoes (or one half can), and chopped basil, parsley and one sprig of thyme. This is added to the rice, and the sausages or oysters, and all is blended well, heated and served together.

Red beans are dried beans. They are soaked over night and the water poured off; they are then cooked with a bit of salt pork, covered with water, adding a tablespoonful of lard, chopped parsley, salt and pepper, and cooked slowly until thick and creamy, and served with rice.

Brown gravies, upon the basis of a brown *roux,* are made thus: To prepare meat in brown gravy take a tablespoonful of pure lard (or butter or margarine for a richer gravy), and melt slowly, being careful not to let it boil. When hot enough to brown a piece of bread dropped into the skillet, it is ready to receive the meat. When the meat has been browned on both sides, remove it from the skillet and set it aside. Now take two tablespoonsful of flour and add slowly to the lard, letting it brown but not scorch. If this should happen you would ruin the *roux.* Add next a cupful of hot water, a proportionate amount of chopped onion, and for added flavor two sprigs of thyme, three of parsley, one bay leaf, or a teaspoonful of dried herbs in this same proportion, a bit of garlic, or garlic salt, a pinch of salt and pepper to taste. Put back the meat and cook slowly for an hour or more, when it will be ready to serve.

You will see how this same beginning is related to the Gumbo. The *roux* is made as above, then are added three quarts of warm water, the herbs and seasonings, and then the crab or shrimp or chicken, which has been previously prepared and *sautéed*. The mixture is boiled slowly for about an hour and a half. If oysters are used they should be dropped into the Gumbo about five minutes before serving. Add two tablespoons of *Filé* a minute or two before serving; it should never be allowed to boil after the *Filé* is added. The bowl of rice is passed at the table after the soup has been served, or a tablespoonful or so may be put in each plate in the serving pantry. Herbs used for the boiling of the crabs were, once upon a time, and now again when we grow them: thyme, bayleaf, allspice, sweet basil, marjoram, mace, chives, parsley, cayenne pepper. When dry herbs are used in cooking, one teaspoonful of the combination will be enough.

Fish is not rationed and is delicious boiled or baked in the Creole way. In baking, the traditional herbs are, one sprig of marjoram, two of thyme, a bit of chervil, parsley, two bay leaves, one blade of mace, for a four-pound fish.

There is more to be told, but space is limited. This does give, however, the foundation upon which can be built the French peasant frugality in cooking which should be useful in these days of rationing. Our New Orleans "Monday wash-day lunches" may now become as famous throughout the land as our Oysters Rockefeller and our Bouillabaisse.

THE AROMATIC LIFE
By MARTHA GENUNG STEARNS

"People who despise the use of a scent-bottle will still agree that the increased cultivation and use of aromatic plants, somewhat after the old manner, but adapted to modern times, would be a gain to health, and certainly preferable to the lavish and increasing use of manufactured scents."

"The Country Housewife's Book." London, 1934

WHEN we think of perfume, we think of the East from whence it came; of aromatic gums and spices, of caravans crossing the Arabian desert to Babylon and its great bazars, bringing musk and bergamot and amber and attar of rose. There is something mysterious about perfume because it speaks to a part of our being which we know least about; it seems related to the spirit rather than the body and it works a spell upon the memory which can transport us in an instant to another time and place. It is real and yet it is indescribable. Incense and prayer have always been linked in Christian worship as well as Pagan: "Let my Prayer, O Lord, be directed as incense in Thy sight."

During the Middle Ages, when the Black Death was raging in Europe, no one knew the correct treatment for that vague menace in the air all around, because no one knew the cause. Every man was his own physician, seeking a cure, and willing to try any theory, hearsay, or magic. The herb garden was heavily drawn upon, not only for herbals remedies to cleanse, purge, heal, but to mask the bad air resulting from tainted matter; what we know today of sanitation, refrigeration, germs and disinfectants was not even suspected in those dreadful years of 1348-50. The most natural thing was to purify the air by burning pine, juniper, cypress and laurel, aloes and amber.

In the abundant knowledge of today, we have a tendency to laugh at the early ideas of medicine and the mediaeval belief in magic. But we lose sight of one important point: the plants really *had* something, then as now. The remedial herbs had definite beneficial properties, not only in their physical effects but in their power of suggestion; and no one should know better than we, in these days when public opinion is so easily swayed, how much suggestion can do to influence the mass mind. Most of the famous old herbalists were physicians and the emphasis in their books is strongly upon the side of the medicinal and beneficial plants rather than the flavoring herbs. Almost everything growing in the old gardens had a useful quality.

As our lives have withdrawn further away from nature we have ceased to be students of natural causes and effects. We live an artificial life; almost everything we use and wear has been produced by some scientific process of tremendous forces of heat and steam working on strange materials. Our foods are preserved with chemicals, our water is purified with them. Our perfumes and flavorings are largely chemical formulas. Even many of our diseases are induced by the conditions under which we live. It is possible that the ancients suffered from appendicitis and rheumatism called by other names, but can we believe that they had the ills resulting from worry, speed, allergies and jitters—in other words, nervous tension? These are a modern product. But still, under our feet there are the same homely little plants and herbs, and it is not unreasonable to think that they can still be efficacious even for modern troubles. Perhaps we are losing something valuable by neglecting them. It is so easy to make a trial.

We are getting accustomed to *ersatz* materials all around us; but there is no such thing as an *ersatz* herb. And if there is magic in the herb garden, it lies in that lovely symphonic chord of fragrances that rises up in the early morning or after a summer rain; in the purely natural act of working down on one's

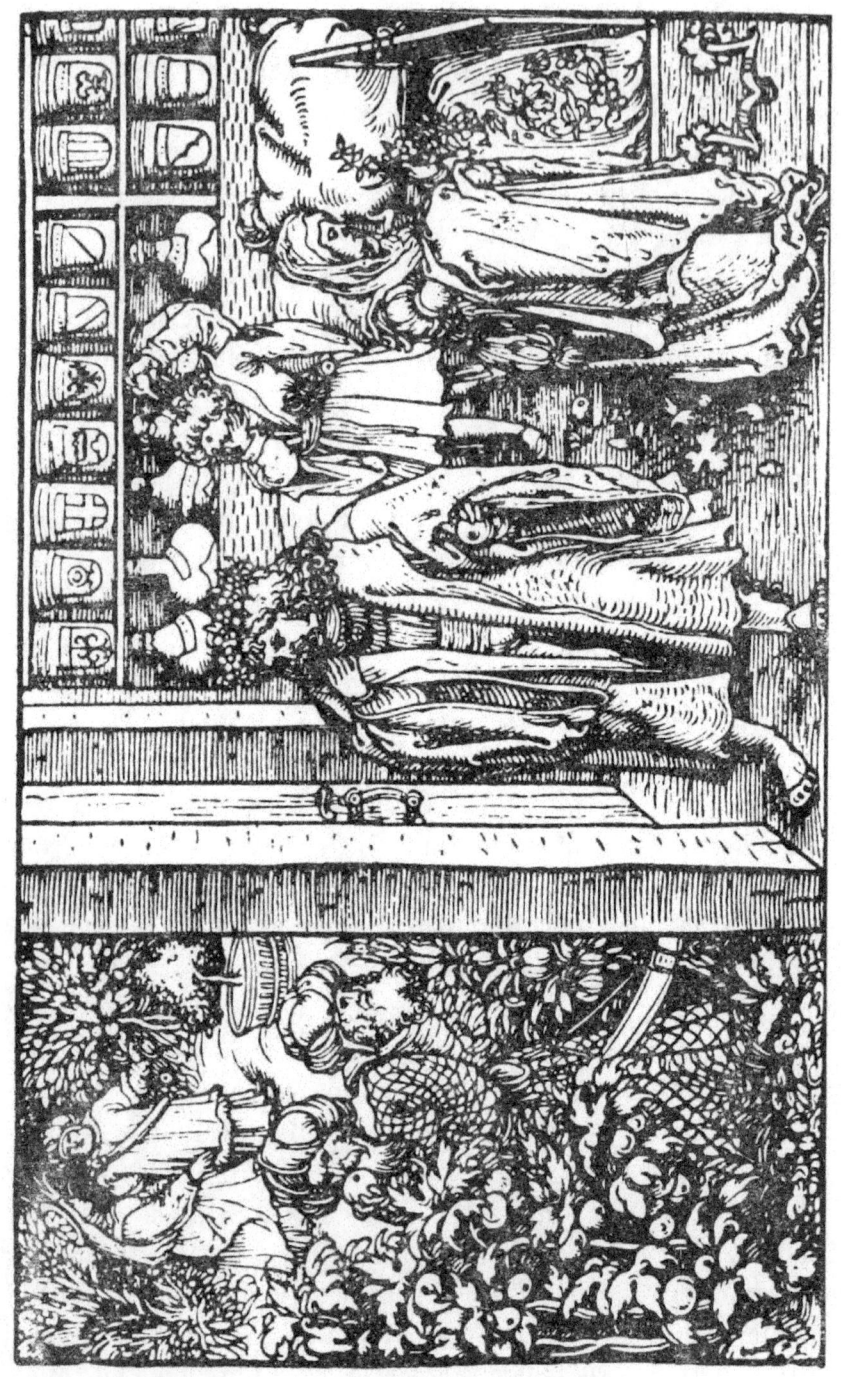

A Herbalist's Garden and Store-room—from Das Kreuterbuch oder Herbarius, printed by Heinrich Steiner, Augsburg, 1534; showing a lady laying sprigs in a linen chest.

knees close to the soil, and breathing in the clean aromatic scents with which we are surrounded. The first cure for tense nerves is right there. Let us consider how this effect can be prolonged by bringing it into the house.

The easiest way is to bring in the cut green herbs, either in a mixed bunch or combined with garden flowers whose bright colors are often enhanced by the neutral foil of herb-foliage. There is the open bowl of dried lavender, which seems to absorb the odors of stale cigar smoke and cooking, renewing its strength if it is shut up for a while. There are the little bags of verbena, rosemary and the fragrant geraniums which we pack away in storage trunks and on the linen shelves; everyone knows these. But there are other easy things to be done without the elaborate process of distilling oils and essences as given in the old stillroom books. They can be practised not for quaint effect, but because they have real practical value, plus the pleasure they give.

Several uses can be found for the oil-laden stems left after your household herbs are stripped. Lemon verbena stalks will hold their fragrance for years if shut away; they can be tied into little fagots for bureau drawers and among the table linen and the bedding, their faint breath stealing out to surprise you. Sage and mint stems, lemon thyme and sweet marjoram and other stems can be cut into pieces and sprinkled over furniture under the dust-covers in a closed house to prevent mustiness. In city apartments where it is difficult to air the things hanging in closets, they can be kept fresher by sweet-bags on the hangers and an apple or orange pomander or two. Dried sweet woodruff is delicious in your hat box; lad'slove with its under-scent of lemon is a pest-preventive. A combination of tansy, wormwood, peppermint, thyme and lavender is recommended to pack away as moths and mice dislike these strong, clean scents, and so a double purpose is served, although for heavy woolens the herbs should be reinforced with camphor or something for added safety. The fruits of the linden attached to their bracts give a delicate scent to a box of letter-paper.

A pad of rose pot-pourri or vetiver can be carried in the suitcase when traveling and left inside it between journeys. Rue, peppermint and costmary strewn green on the floor of an automobile will temper a long, hot ride; a sprig or two in your handbag on a train will give you something new to think about. In very hot weather the green herbs give a suggestion of clean coolness. In fact, why not try the old Elizabethan practise of "strewing" on your porch, to let the passing feet press the odors from green sprigs? They are easily swept up.

In the winter, sprinkle dried southernwood in a pan on a hot register, or throw a bit of pot-pourri on a stove; put herb-scented water into the radiator-thermidor. Heat a shovel in the hot ashes in the fireplace and sprinkle juniper berries and rosemary and herbal odds and ends on it for a sort of domestic incense. It is a good end for last year's dried things when you replace with a new harvest, to mix them with pinecones for kindling the fire.

There are many toilet uses for the fragrant herbs. A cheesecloth bag of them (green) can be put into a hot bath which releases their odor; these herbal baths and soothing herbal teas just before bedtime are recommended by tired war-workers in England. The fresh loose sprigs could be used except for the difficulty of their getting in the drain. After a home shampoo, rub rose-geranium leaves between your hands as you dry and handle your hair. A camomile rinse is a very good softener, especially for blond hair. Orris root, the base of so many perfumes, is so hard when dried that it is difficult to powder finely at home; but a small piece as a "washing ball" retains its odor for a long time.

For sick people in hospitals, a definite use can be found for small herbal pads and pillows to counteract the smells of medicine, ether and disinfectants, and also to induce pleasant thoughts and drowsiness. The flowers of everlasting and leaves of beech will absorb the herb scents and give bulk in these pillows. As mint and thyme are among the ingredients of the inhalers sold for colds, the fresh herbs can do something toward clearing the breathing, and have the charm of novelty in a hospital. It is not hard to make scented rubbing-alcohol by steeping bay, bergamot and the lemon plants in the spirits.

We must never forget that the blind, who miss so much of the color and texture of flowers, can enjoy aromatic scents to the full, and find an intense interest and pleasure in the fragrant herbs. They learn to identify the very individual scents of rue, sweetmary, the different mints and geraniums, lemon balm, pennyroyal. For sheer sweetness many love the rose geranium best, but agree that there is something exciting about rue with its half-bitter, half-sweet, wholly clean odor, a sense of purification. To the sick who must get through long hours, these small things become great and bring more pleasure than we realize.

Each of us must have made some pleasant discovery to add to this simple list, which may help inquirers to learn what to do with their herb garden. There is a homely delight in living an aromatic life in an aromatic house, and nature's own perfumes are never too strong.

THE CIMARUTA, A NEAPOLITAN GOOD-LUCK AMULET

A SILVER "Cimaruta" pendant, or sprig of rue (from *Cima,* top or summit, and *Ruta,* rue), bears among its branches eight good-luck symbols, partly Christian and partly pagan in origin. From its association with rue, or sorrow, the plant became the symbol of repentance, the Herb of Grace, and has always been connected with the idea of protection from evil fortune, disease, insects, and witchcraft. Though bitter it was much used in cooking and in flavoring wine, and had medicinal properties given in the old Herbals. A sprig of rue was often used to sprinkle holy water in the blessing of houses, was hung up in law courts to keep away jail fever, and was one of the Elizabethan strewing-herbs used in houses and hospitals because of its clean pungent scent.

HOME MADE INKS
By CATHERINE H. SWEENEY

"MODERN ink is a mixture of a tannic decoction with a solution of copperas." This statement sounds simple but the history of ink manufacture belies that simplicity. The chemical formulas of our most common inks have been developed through centuries of fascinating experimentation.

Since many good inks can be made by an amateur, let us make a study of some of these formulas or recipes, with an emphasis on the native plant life, a newly revived interest which unfolds to us a wide field of outdoor study.

David N. Carvalho, in FORTY CENTURIES of INK, speaks of the background of our writing fluids. The Hebrew ink was "a simple mixture of powdered charcoal or soot with water, to which gum was sometimes added." The Arabians and Chinese had more complex inks, but also based on carbon (charcoal or soot). These carbon-based inks are today grouped together as the "India" inks. Then there is a miscellaneous group of writing fluids, all of which have a most interesting history, such as the sepia, the protective fluid of the cuttlefish, which yielded a brown liquid, and other inks of organic pigments, the pokeberry, for instance, which I shall mention later. They are simply a coloring matter in water. The greatest number of inks, including our commercial ones, are the tannic-copperas compound fluids. These are more difficult to make at home, but can be done by the amateur.

The peasantry of the European world and our own ancestors upon this continent used home made inks for their letters and documents as well as home made dyes for their fabrics. They had an ample supply of plant resources upon which to draw, and they learned to use that supply most ingeniously; and we are again learning to use some of these plants, not only due to possible shortages but as a matter of genuine interest in the fields and forests about us. One of the most interesting volumes on the use of native materials, written because of war shortages in the Southern States, in 1863, is *Resources of Southern Fields*, by F. P. Porcher, published first at Richmond, later at Charleston. *American Weeds* and *Useful Plants*, by William Darlington, 1859, is another splendid early book on exploring our outdoors. Ernest Thompson Seton's *Woodcraft Manual for Boys* gives at least one ink recipe. There are many other volumes dealing with primitive dyestuffs and pigments but which do not actually give ink formulas. Among these, I might mention *Useful Wild Plants of the United States and Canada*, by C. F. Saunders, 1920.

Let us take up the so-called "miscellaneous" inks first. They are more simple.

The pokeberry (Phytolacca americana), has berries of a deep purple color which can be crushed and the juice used either fresh or boiled. The juice does not have to be reduced in volume, but the color is fugitive — that is, the beautiful color fades to a brown if kept in a liquid state. The writer has, however, been able to retain the color by allowing the liquid to evaporate entirely, and then adding water when needed. Porcher found that alum added to the juice kept the color. He also suggested that the berries be boiled with sugar, and with a little alcohol and alum they would make a good ink.

Saunders writes of Indian use of the Rocky Mountain Bee Plant (Cleome serrulata) "The plants are collected in summer, boiled down thoroughly, and the thick black residual fluid then allowed to dry and harden in cakes. Pieces of this are soaked in hot water when needed to paint." Presumably this might be a possible ink.

Carvalho quotes Pliny as saying that indigo (Indigofera tinctoria), occasionally found in old gardens, was used as a very permanent ink, but that he, Pliny, had not yet investigated it. Indigo has until recently been added occasionally to commercial inks, but artificial dyes have superceded it.

Of inky-cap mushrooms (Coprinus stramentarius and C. micaceus) Porcher says: "The deliquescent fungi might be prepared into an excellent India ink, and its dried deposit, mixed with oil, might probably answer for engravings."

Tannic acid, or tannin, is one of the components of commercial as well as home made ink when combined with copperas. This tannin with copperas produces a finely divided black precipitate. It is produced by a number of American woody plants. Tannin is prepared especially from oak galls, which are an abnormal growth on oak trees developed by those plants through the irritation caused by the depositing of parasitic insect eggs in plant tissue. The tannin in the galls is changed through a fermentation process into gallic acid. However the oak galls are not the only sources of tannin.

Darlington speaks of the sumacs, (Rhus glabra and R. typhina), used for tanning purposes, and that European varieties are used in calico printing and in dyeing Morocco leather.

Seton gives only one recipe for home made ink, that of the sumac. He suggests that the berries and the leaves be boiled together, to give a permanent blue-black ink. This writer has boiled the berries of the staghorn sumac, but found only a muddy brown liquid, even after "boiling it down."

Porcher writes that the juice of poison ivy, (Rhus toxicodendron), a relative of the sumacs, makes a good indelible ink. This writer is inclined to believe that the experience with poison ivy might be somewhat more indelible on one's memory than on paper. Porcher also mentions the flowering dogwood (Cornus florida) as yielding tannin of ink-making quality.

Tannin is also produced by the maples (Acer sp.) and we find Porcher gives two recipes for their use. One of these combines maple bark with pine needles (Pinus sp.) and copperas, sugar and vinegar. The second combines maple bark with the barks of white oak (Quercus alba) and red oak (Quercus rubra) to which is added copperas. According to Darlington, the bark of the red maple "affords a dark purplish-blue dye and makes a pretty good bluish black ink." This is Acer rubrum.

Porcher gives still another combination of native plants, utilizing the red oak with elderberries, (Sambucus canadensis), although elderberries can be used alone with copperas and alum.

The persimmon (Diospyros virginiana) contains much tannin, especially in the unripe fruit, of which Porcher and others have written. There are several short monographs on the subject of tannin in persimmons, which proves some interest in the subject. Porcher's recipe is as follows: "12 green persimmons, mashed; pour on enough water to cover them. Boil over a slow fire, but not too much, add in a piece of copperas. This ink will not change color and cannot be washed or rubbed out."

Lastly, the fig (Ficus sp.) contains some coloring matter—a red pigment in the skins, while the pomegranate (Punica granatum) which is hardly a native field flower, but might be available to some of us, yields a fine black ink, according to both Porcher and Carvalho. The latter states that pomegranate ink was used as early as the eighth century A. D.

Several plants with which we are familiar have common names which might mislead the amateur to try them for ink. The inkberry (Ilex glabra) is one of these, and the other is Inkroot (Statice limonium), which is unusable even though it does contain twelve percent tannic acid.

Besides, there are many native dyes mentioned by all these authors that might make a faint colored ink, but would not ordinarily be considered of true ink quality. I have not listed these.

We can experiment upon our own yards and fields, and find for ourselves not only a useful article but the satisfaction of unusual achievement.

THE INTER-AMERICAN QUININE PROGRAM

THE story of quinine is more than three hundred years old and has often been told. But it assumes new significance today, when thousands of servicemen from temperate climates are being sent out to fever-ridden jungles. More than that, quinine is a world-need, in a world where 4,000,000 lives a year are taken by malaria from the Five Continents and the Seven Seas. Many countries are now linked in the production of enough quinine to relieve the shortage caused by the seizure of Java by Japan, and their scientists are working in close cooperation. It is truly a weapon of defense, common to all, for it remains the most effective anti-malarial drug known. It kills the malarial parasite in both the mosquito which carries the disease, and the mosquito's host — a preventive and a cure.

Quinine must be grown; it cannot be made. From a very tiny seed, 75,000 to the ounce, the cinchona plant must reach a height of 3 feet before its bark can be tested for its alkaloid content, and it is seven more years before the new trees in turn bear seed. The method of harvesting, which is the same now as that employed by the Indians hundreds of years ago, is to cut down the tree and strip its bark, which is ground into powder. Mature cinchona trees produce about 8 tons of bark to an acre, or 16,000 pounds of quinine.

The curative properties of cinchona bark were learned from the Indians of Peru by Spanish explorers and by the Jesuit missionaries who took it back to Europe, where it was first called "Jesuit bark." As explorations and conquests grew and white men penetrated further into tropical regions, it became more and more important, and until after 1860 practically all of the supply came from Latin America. Today, not even the newly discovered synthetic anti-malarial drugs can take its place, and the Army uses only pure quinine for our soldiers in the tropics.

Cinchona Seedlings at Plant Introduction Garden, Glendale, Maryland.
Courtesy of the U. S. Department of Agriculture

As we review the whole story of the drug, a panorama of surprising breadth opens out, involving many countries, and some outstanding figures who have built from very small beginnings.

It is due first to an Englishman, Charles Ledger, that the field began to widen. In 1854 he discovered a high-yielding strain of cinchona in Bolivia which received his name, Ledgeriana, and he sent about 14 pounds of selected seed to London in the hope of introducing its commercial cultivation in some of Britain's tropical colonies. At that time, however, no one in England was sufficiently impressed by its importance to take up the work. It was the Dutch, with their tropical possessions, who were more far-seeing and bought one pound of the seed for $100. From this small beginning they started the industry in Java, which has been the source of 95% of the world's best supply — until Pearl Harbor. The drug must pass a fixed standard, and the Javanese variety, descended from cinchona Ledgeriana, showed up more evenly than the wild cinchona native to the slopes of the Andes in which the quality varies with the tree and cannot be determined without almost individual tests.

When the war rushed upon us, changing the whole aspect of the Pacific, a plan was set in motion by the United States to reach every available source of quinine and to develop a new supply. Vice-President Wallace, the head of the former Office of Economic Warfare, collaborated with foreign diplomats and with technicians from the Office of Foreign Agricultural Relations, and men were mobilized for the work with all the grim determination of real battle.

The Latin American countries were naturally unwilling to strip their own supply down to the danger point, but they were more than willing to help in the establishment of large plantations on their soil, with American assistance. However, the seed then available was not the Ledgeriana strain, but of an inferior quality.

Early in 1942, Colonel A. F. Fischer of the U. S. Army was

very ill of malaria in the field hospital on Bataan, and the quinine supply was practically gone. Colonel Fischer had previously been head of the Philippine Bureau of Forestry and had started an experimental plantation of the better strain of cinchona on the island of Mindanao. In spite of his grave condition, he managed to fly there, and by improvising some crude equipment started to produce the drug. This was just before the fall of Bataan, which brought the immediate prospect of the Philippines falling into Japanese hands. Colonel Fischer succeeded in gathering several million seeds, with the help of his Filipino workers, packed them into sealed cans and flew them to the United States. They were brought to the Department of Agriculture's experimental station at Glendale, Maryland, just outside of Washington.

All sorts of handicaps had to be overcome before all the arrangements for the growing were completed; but now a gigantic program for the producing of cinchona is well under way. The planting of the seed and development of propagation methods has been most successfully carried out under the direction of Mr. Benjamin Y. Morrison, Chief of the Division of Plant Exploration since 1934.

A staff of 20 experienced tropical horticulturalists watch the seedlings like expert doctors and nurses, check temperature, measure water, and treat them like delicate infants until they are about 18 inches high at 6 months old. As the time comes for moving them, the plants are put on a regimen of cooler temperature and less water. Then they are wrapped in sphagnum moss and packed into cartons to be shipped by air to their tropical destinations in Costa Rica, Peru, Ecuador, Mexico, Brazil, Salvador, Puerto Rico, Nicaragua and Colombia. Upon arrival, they are set out in a plantation nursery until they have started growth and established more roots, when they are set in their permanent locations. Thousands of acres of the young trees from Glendale are now flourishing in the midst of the tropical forests under the equator, and as this is written, Mr. Morrison is on a tour of inspection of his far-flung stations in South America.

In the meanwhile, plans call for the shipment of over 100,000 more plants within the next few months, for as the trees must be cut down when stripped, a new supply of seedlings must be kept coming. There is enough now in sight, it is believed, to provide an adequate supply of quinine for our war needs. And this inter-American program should help very materially to relieve the world shortage and build up a reserve supply for postwar needs. Here is one more of the countless enterprises in all departments of work which are bound up together in the American war effort.

From material released by the Foreign Plant Introduction Station, U. S. Department of Agriculture.

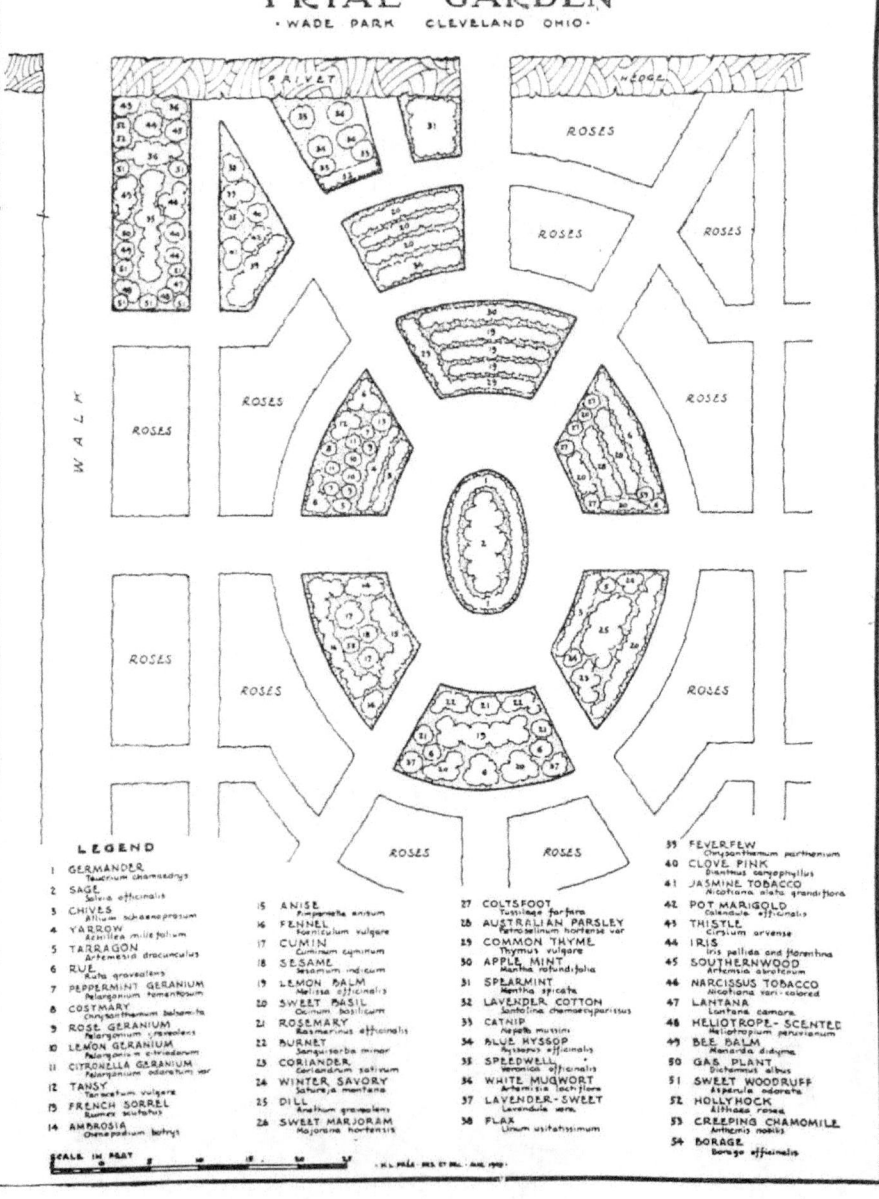

HERBS FOR CLEVELAND
By LUCILE M. BOETHELT, M.A.

WE know what fine herbs are grown in New England. Many people here have claimed to grow fine herbs, and now we know they do. For two years we have had a trial garden composed of donations of perennials and gifts of the seeds. Now it is a real part of the Cleveland Park Department plan. Mr. Henry L. Pree transcribed the design, which already exists in the rose garden. Japanese beetles have been hard on the roses, but our sturdy herbs have resisted their attacks — the survival of the fittest, we hope — and next year the plots marked roses in the plan will be filled with herbs. The legend shows the varieties which are already growing here.

Cumin seed germinated and has grown lustily. The family characteristics are not present, and we account for it as due to the fact that the seed came from India, and often "environment changes the whole nature of the plant," says Dr. J. Paul Visscher of Western Reserve University. We have given a plant to the Botany Department of the University in hopes that the plant will set seed and complete the cycle in this climate.

Mrs. A. R. Boethelt, Chairman Western Reserve Unit, H. S. A.

RECIPES WITH A DIFFERENCE

TO the cautious cook experimenting with herb seasonings, we suggest that herbs are used not so much for their food value as for their appetizer value; and this is conveyed partly by their fragrance in cooking. Heat and liquid release the flavor and odor, and if the pinch of herbs is added to the dish long enough before it is done to bring out these qualities, it is only necessary to use a small quantity. An appetizing smell whets the expectant appetite and aids in good digestion. The savory herbs should not mask the flavor of the dish but only add to it a reminder of themselves.

Dr. Roberta Ma, Assistant to Dr. William J. Robbins of the New York Botanical Garden, who is an authority on Chinese matters, says: "Chinese people eat more green vegetables than any other people, vegetables which have high vitamin content, as follows: fresh or dried soy beans, green beans, cabbage of many varieties, celery, lettuce, celtuce, peas, spinach, dandelion, watercress (Wing-tsai-Tung-ho), gourds, tubers, turnips, carrots, etc. The following is a recipe for using the flowers of hemerocallis fulva in soup:

1. Fresh buds (just before opening) for six, 2 cups cut or left whole.
   4 cups of meat broth
   $1\frac{1}{2}$ cups of meat or chicken
   Salt to taste
   Cook meat in broth until tender; add salt, then the buds; cook for a few minutes before serving.

2. Dried buds.
   Similar to above, but cook dried buds and meat together until both are tender, add salt and some green vegetables, such as watercress or cabbage leaves, cook a few minutes longer."

The Garden Chairman of the Washington Unit, American Women's Voluntary Services, recommends the following recipes for using wild fruits.

Wild Strawberry Leather:— Take thoroughly ripe berries, mash to a pulp, spread on platters and dry in the sun or a very slow oven. When dry, dust with powdered sugar and roll up like a jelly cake and cut. (The rolling is for convenience in handling and storing). This "leather" was eaten either as a confection or soaked in water and used for pies, shortcake, sauces or tarts. The author highly recommends this but warns that cheesecloth should be put over mash if dried in the sun, to keep out insects.

Rose Hip Jam:— Choose species of rose that has large fruits, called hips in America, haws in England. Remove seeds. Allow half a pint of water to each pound of ripe hips and boil until they are quite tender. Then rub through a sieve and to each pound of the pulp allow a pound of sugar and boil until it is stiff.

Elderberry Chutney:— To 2 pounds of cleaned elderberries, slightly crushed, add one large onion chopped up, a pint of vinegar, a teaspoon of salt, a teaspoon of ground ginger, two teaspoons (or more) of sugar, $1/4$ teaspoon each of pepper and mixed spices. Bring to a boil and simmer until thick. Stir frequently. Pour into hot jars and seal.

Herb Sandwiches:— Spread with butter whole thin slices of fresh bread, either white, whole wheat or oatmeal, home made if possible. Snip up finely with scissors one part each of parsley, chives, lovage, basil, to a half-part each of savory, mint and sage. At the time of serving, let each one sprinkle the herbs on the bread and fold it over.

A member of the Society recommends frying whole sage leaves in the pan with sausages until crisp.

Another member has the following way of heating baked beans, especially recommended for reviving canned beans: Put a layer of beans in a deep casserole, cover with raw onion, chopped or sliced, a layer of tomato, fresh or canned, and sprinkle with savory. Repeat, with savory all through, and bake two hours in a slow oven.

A fried delicacy:— Pick off some of the superfluous buds from a squash vine just before they open, and fry in deep fat until delicately brown. Serve hot as a garnish.

VEGETABLES PREPARED FOR PETS
By FRANCES R. WILLIAMS

REALIZING that vegetables might be scarce and expensive in war-time, I canned for my dog's food the green tops or leaves cut off the carrots which I had canned for table use. To mix well with the rest of the dog's food, I cut the carrot tops very fine with scissors; this is a necessary step, as otherwise the pieces of stem would act as an emetic. A letter from the U. S. Department of Agriculture states that carrot tops would be a good source of calcium and of the vitamin riboflavin, and a rich source of vitamin A. Consequently they make an excellent element in the dog's diet.

The next year, I canned more carrot tops, the coarse beet tops, and some second grade cabbage, by the same recipe used to can any greens.

I know of a cat which is very partial to canned peas, which take many ration points from the ration book of its mistress. As an alternative, I suggested that some catnip be cooked with carrots, and this the cat condescended to eat. About $\frac{1}{4}$ cup of catnip was used with one cup of carrots. Such a combination might be canned to help solve food problems with other cats. Dry catnip might be sprinkled on food; as in the case of all herbs, it should stand a little while to bring out the flavor.

SOME BOOKS OF THE PAST YEAR WITH HERBAL INTEREST

The printing issued by the Metropolitan Museum of Art is always done with distinction, and "Herbs for the Mediaeval Household," by Margaret B. Freeman, is a notable example. For those unfamiliar with herb literature it is a pleasant introduction to mediaeval herbals, and to those who know the plants it is a refreshing compilation of over fifty well known herbs, illustrated with woodcuts for the most part from the "Hortus Sanitatis" published by Peter Schoeffer at Maintz in 1485. The mediaeval housewife is not ridiculed in the light of our modern sophistication, and yet her remedies are not given without a guiding touch by the author, who gives each one its modern notation, and quotes, "Most of the remedies I am confident are true, and if there be any that are not so, yet they are pleasant." Every book-lover would enjoy owning this 48-page volume, but the first edition is limited to 2600 copies, price $1.50.

A workmanlike little volume has been written by Dr. E. D. Merrill, Director of the Arnold Arboretum and Honorary President of the Herb Society. It is issued by the U. S. War Department for the use of our fighting men and entitled "Emergency Food Plants and Poisonous Plants of the Islands of the Pacific," and is the right size to be carried handily in the pocket. The greater part of the plants listed and illustrated are edible in an emergency; there are sections on edible ferns, palms, tubers, fruits and seeds, etc., and in some cases their medicinal properties are given. Two chapters at the end cover the poisonous and harmful plants likely to be found; but Dr. Merrill is reassuring and says that the number of really dangerous poisons is small. He adds that "the widespread fear of the snake-infested jungle" is the result of too much stress on an entirely imaginary picture of the Malayan region.

A similar handbook has been prepared for the U. S. Navy by the Smithsonian Institution and gives some instructions about plant foods, edible fungi and roots. It dwells more particularly on the stars, island survival, signal fires, and much helpful advice to shipwrecked sailors. Its title is "Survival on Land and Sea," and it is not for sale to the general public.

David Fairchild, in "Garden Islands of the Great East," has written an account of his expedition to collect seeds in the Philippines and Netherlands India which reads like a romance or a dream. At Manila he joined the Junk "Cheng Ho," — "her picturesque henna-colored sails all set, the sun illuminating the gorgeous gilded and painted carvings of her stern and sides," for the voyage to Java, Celebes and the Moluccas, the results of which may be to bring some exotic plant to our own gardens as a familiar friend. We have here much scientific knowledge, stories of the friendships between learned men all over the world, and wonderful intimate photographs of strange things. (Scribner, 1943).

"Edible Wild Plants of Eastern North America," a special publication of the Gray Herbarium at Harvard by its Director, Professor Merritt Lyndon Fernald, and Professor Alfred Charles Kinsey of Indiana University (Idlewild Press, 1943) is a fascinating book. The authors look for their public first among the lovers of outdoors and of camping in the wilds (and who hasn't his occasional primitive-man moods?), and next among thoughtful people who are already wondering what will happen to our world food supply in the years to come.

The book takes the form of a fanciful cook-book, and suggests native menus "from soup to nuts." There are chapters on purées and soups, bready vegetables and salads, relishes, drinks, syrups, as well as mushrooms and seaweeds; and a few poisonous plants are described which are likely to be mistaken for useful ones. Every plant has its technical Latin name known to all scientists; but its colloquial name may be regional, like squaw-huckleberry, cow parsnip, mayflower, and it needs careful description; and here are useful drawings and a fine index. Many plants mentioned are already installed in our herb gardens—corn salad, pennyroyal, chicory—but the uses of many others perhaps still need to be learned, like the common spikenard, which "has great possibilities." Everyone can learn more about our wild plants, and we are looking forward to a meeting with the Perplexing Hypholoma, and to pinching the root of Sedum Rosea to see if it really smells like attar-of-roses.

Mrs. Helen Morgenthau Fox's book, "Gardening for Good Eating," published in 1943, was previewed in the Herbarist No. 9, 1943, in which we were privileged to have an article by herself.

A Few Booklets and Catalogues—

"Selected Recipes with Culinary Herbs," a small cookbook of recipes contributed for the use of "Bundles for America," to be sold for the relief of the dependent families of our service men. Price 1.00. Many well known names appear among the contributors.

A Collection of Creole Recipes as Used in New Orleans. This comes from Kiskatom Farm and gives many uses for culinary herbs, including the famous *Filé* powder made from sassafras. Price 1.00.

"It is Easy to Grow Herbs," a handbook of information by Bunny and Phil Foster of Laurel Hill Herb Farm, Morristown, N. J. This booklet gives a very good list of herb seeds obtainable, home grown and fresh. Price 25 cents.

FIELD NOTES

Herbarium in Swinging Frames.— Dartmouth College is the recipient of a fine herbarium of the plants of northern New England, presented by Miss Elizabeth Billings of Woodstock, Vermont. The collection, which is the work of many years, has been placed in the Wilson Museum at Hanover, N. H., and the sheets of mounted plants are filed under glass in specially constructed upright frames which makes it possible to look through the entire collection with ease. This will be much used by New England botanists north of Boston.

Stinging Nettles for the War.— English schoolchildren, working barelegged and barehanded in the fields collecting great quantities of nettles, have apparently proved the truth of the old adage about grasping the nettle firmly. Gathering herbs is a village industry; the work of drying and stripping is done by the women, and brick and pottery works closed down by the war are used as drying places, the leaves being spread on light frames covered with old net or muslin curtains. The stalks and leaves are used for making a special kind of paper.

Helping the Milk Supply.— A new application of a well known drug comes in the news from England, which may have great importance for the country's milk supply. The dreaded cattle disease mastitis causes such slow deterioration of a cow and the quality of its milk that a whole herd can be infected before it is discovered. The drug Aesculin, derived from the fresh bark of the horse chestnut tree, is now being used to detect the presence of the disease early; by "cultivating" a sample of milk from the suspected cow and adding aesculin to it, the infection can be proved before it spreads.

Notes from the West Coast.— We learn of constant development in Washington and Oregon where digitalis and cascara are indigenous, in the cultivation of scarce drugs and herbs. Labor shortage had reduced the gathering of the wild supply from this natural source; but the difference in temperature, rainfall and soil on both sides of the Cascade range makes it an ideal growing ground to cultivate many plants of varying requirements successfully. Peppermint, belladonna, stramonium (golden seal) and lavender have been cultivated in large acreage. The commercial nature of the project, however, precludes any educational value, such as the keeping of records on soil, fertilizer and labor costs would give us. Artemisia cina-levant (worm seed) is also cultivated successfully, but as it is largely a monopoly, seeds and plants are not readily available for experimental purposes.

Florida: Swamps Made Productive.— The Florida Everglades, so long considered an unproductive waste area, is now contributing to the war effort. The U. S. Sugar Corporation is producing sugarcane over some 30,000 acres which gives not only thousands of bags of raw brown sugar but a by-product of more than 4,000,000 gallons of blackstrap molasses. The latter is used in certain kinds of cattle-food, taking the place of a considerable quantity of corn. Another new product of the Everglades is lemongrass, the oil from which is between 75 and 80 per cent pure citrol. When the oil has been extracted, the dehydrated grass pulp is combined with the molasses and some proteins are added to form a ration for cattle, thus tying both these industries together.

TWO INSECT PESTS
By HELEN NOYES WEBSTER

IT IS with no flight of the imagination that I remember that twenty years ago the herbs planted in various parts of my yard were free from pests, both fungus and insect. The mints did not rust, rosemary leaves did not curl with mites, parsnip webworm let the flowering umbels of angelica alone and its fertile seed covered the ground with seedlings every spring.

It was then that I blithely wrote, "The herb garden is a joyous thing free from pests." Today I say, "Watch out," and I keep the dusters well filled with derris, nicotine and pyrethrum. What has happened? Has the increasing popularity of herb gardening and increased planting of herbs provided new forage grounds for the bugs and new hosts for the fungi? Certainly things are different amongst the herbs. That fat green and black banded celery worm—*papilio polyxenes* to the entomologist—now chews away on rows of dill and fennel, but he is a minor pest, so easily picked off that the use of precious deterrent is a waste of material.

An insect, almost microscopically small, and which looks for all the world like a tiny crab, two summers ago laid low a flourishing patch of costmary, and then took as a side dish a neighboring bed of camphor plant. *Chrysanthemum balsamita*. To weed among these herbs with bare arms was torture for the miserable little pests swarmed over every inch of bare skin with nipping bites which itched for hours. A few years ago I would have said that nothing could daunt the vigorous spread of these herbs, but I reckoned without this voracious insect, which left only etiolated stems, yellow dried leaves and discouraged bloom in its wake.

Professor W. D. Whitcomb, entomological authority of the Waltham (Mass.) Field Station, identified the insect as the goldenrod lacebug, *Corythuca marmorata*. Its traditional feeding grounds are among the asters and ornamental composites of the flower garden, which it left for fresher and more novel fields. Professor Whitcomb suggested a spray of wettable derris, three tablespoonfuls to a gallon of water with one tablespoonful of soap flakes. This helped, but I took no chance and burned the whole bed to the ground; even then I found that prevention must begin with the first showing of leaves from the root stocks, which were kept well dusted with pyrethrum.

Last summer in early June, the lovage leaves which at this time should be at the height of their succulence, began to shrivel and turn brown. Stems were stunted and few plants bloomed. Specimens which were hurried over to Professor Whitcomb elicited an interesting reply: "The specimens of lovage are attacked by the parsnip leaf miner, known scientifically as *Acidia fratria*. It is occasionally seen on parsnip but this is the first report that I have received of its attacking lovage."

About this time a near by bed of angelica likewise became infested. Examination of the larger leaves showed maggots of the miner embedded in the soft internal tissues, particularly along the midribs and larger veins. It was evident that I should have caught the adult fly before it bored into the leaf to lay eggs from which these maggots hatched. To quote further from Professor Whitcomb's letter, "No simple satisfactory control of this insect is known; it helps to spray with nicotine sulfate in the proportion of 2 teaspoonfuls in a gallon of water. This kills the young maggots of related species of leaf miners if applied when the miners are very small. To be effective, the spray must be applied at the proper time which must be determined by observation."

It was encouraging to learn in the course of a conversation with him that this pest was not common; it had appeared for the first time on angelica at the Field Station and weather conditions might not favor its reappearance here for twenty years. However, I took no chances, and all angelica and lovage were cut to the ground. Burning, last year at least, was cheaper than insecticides; and before the ground thaws there will be another cleansing with a light burning of leaves spread over the herb patches. If possible, the location of the beds will be changed to conceal their whereabouts from the lacebug and the miner.

The HERBARIST *for* 1944

A Limited Edition
Written and Published by

THE HERB SOCIETY *of* AMERICA

Price $1.00

A few copies of previous years are still available at $1.00 each

Other publications of the Herb Society of America

BELLADONNA. Reprint from the Herbarist. (1941).	.25
RECORDS OF A GROUP OF SAGE GROWERS. (1942).	.25
THE HOME GROWING OF TWELVE CONDIMENT HERBS. Second Edition. (1942).	.25
THE USE AND METHODS OF MAKING AN HERBARIUM. (1942).	.25
THE COTTAGE HERB INDUSTRY. Reprint from Herbarist. (1943).	.15
SAGE BULLETIN NO. 3, INCLUDING NEW FERTILIZER TESTS. (1943).	.25
SAGE BULLETIN NO. 4, INCLUDING CONTINUED FERTILIZER TESTS. (1944).	.25

Free Publications:

SOME SOURCES OF HERB SEEDS, PLANTS, AND DRIED PRODUCTS, Information Sheet No. 5. (1942).
A SUGGESTED READING LIST OF HERBS, Information Sheet No. 6. (1943).

Address

THE HERB SOCIETY *of* AMERICA
HORTICULTURAL HALL

300 Massachusetts Avenue　　　　　　Boston, Massachusetts

OUR CONTRIBUTORS
MARTHA GENUNG STEARNS, *Editor*

DR. GILBERT GROSVENOR is the President of the National Geography Society and has been Editor-in-Chief of the National Geographic Magazine since 1903. His life interest has been geography in all its branches, and the list of his college degrees, citations and honors is very long. It was from the Grosvenor home in Baddeck, Cape Breton Island, that his brother-in-law, David Fairchild, started on the seed-gathering expedition described in his latest book.

MRS. A. R. BOETHELT, Chairman of the Western Reserve Unit of the Herb Society, is enthusiastically introducing herbs to Cleveland in many ways. The herb booth superintended by her at the Harvest Festival there was awarded a blue ribbon. Mrs. Boethelt took her Master's degree from Cornell.

MRS. CAROLINE D. WEISS of Kiskatom Farm near New Orleans is growing and processing herbs and studying their history at the same time, thereby doing much to educate the public in their uses.

MRS. FRANCES R. WILLIAMS was awarded a medal and blue ribbon for her exhibit of canned foods for pets at a Victory Garden show last August.

MRS. EDWARD C. SWEENEY is the Victory Garden Chairman of the American Women's Voluntary Services in Washington, D. C., and a most successful gardener. She took her B. S. degree from the University of Illinois in geology, and did graduate work in zoology at the University of Arizona, and also has the distinction of being one of very few women to qualify as a Nature Guide in the Yosemite School of Field Natural History.

MR. B. Y. MORRISON, although not the author of the article on Cinchona production, is Chief of the Division of Plant Exploration and Introduction and directed the work at Glendale, and is a distinguished member of the Herb Society.

MRS. HOLLIS WEBSTER, who warns us of the dismal prospect of pests on herbs, is the author of "Herbs, How to Grow Them and How to Use Them," and too well known to need further introduction to our readers.

THE COLLECTOR'S DREAM

In a recent catalogue from an English book seller there is an item which shows what it is that keeps people still searching the dealer's catalogues and dusty shelves in mingled hope and despair. There is only one copy of this in existence:

"HAPPE, A. F. Herbarium Pictum, sive Icones CCCCII Plantarum officinalium et hortensium ad vivum depictarum. Manuscript, c. 1780. 4 volumes. Folio.

A magnificent Herbal containing a complete series of 402 most carefully executed and coloured drawings of plants after nature. Every plant is given its Latin and French name and the Linnean nomenclature, and the whole series is numbered consecutively from 1-402. Very many plants have a description in French on a separate sheet giving their flowering time, characteristics and properties. The painting is done in bright and effective albumen colours, and since every representation is protected by a contemporary sheet of thin paper, the state of preservation and the freshness of the colouring leave nothing to be desired.

These volumes comprise the *oeuvre* of the Berlin botanist, Andreas F. Happe, used in the publication of a number of botanical portfolios issued by him between 1783-1792, (see Pritzel 4121-4). According to the MS title-page, on which Happe is described as "defunctus," these volumes must have been compiled after his death. The front cover of each volume bears a label on which is written "Herbier artificiel coloré par de Happe, composé de 402 figures."

THE HERB SOCIETY OF AMERICA
OFFICERS AND DIRECTORS
1943 - 1944

OFFICERS

President-at-Large	Dr. E. D. Merrill
President	Mrs. John H. Cunningham
Vice-president	Mrs. A. C. Burrage Jr.
2nd Vice-president	Mrs. Foster Stearns
Secretary	Mrs. Laurence A. Brown
Treasurer	Miss Margaret Norton

STANDING COMMITTEES

Botanical Research and Bibliography	Mrs. Hollis Webster
Curator of Herbarium and Publicity	Mrs. Frances R. Williams
Commercial Research and Publication Committee	Mrs. E. B. Cole
The Herbarist	Mrs. Foster Stearns, *Editor*

DIRECTORS

Mrs. Pierce Archer	Mrs. John Gibbon
Mrs. Arthur B. Baer	Mrs. Alfred Kay
Mrs. G. Page Ely	Mrs. E. L. Mitchell
Mrs. Robert Fife	Mrs. Alfred Stengel
Miss E. Van Brunt	Mrs. Spencer Thorpe
Mrs. Donald Durant	Mrs. H. H. Richards

Mr. and Mrs. Sherman K. Hardy

UNIT CHAIRMEN

Philadelphia:
  Mrs. John H. Gibbon, Lynfield Farm, Media, Penna.
New York:
  Miss Elizabeth Remson Van Brunt, Kitchawan, N. Y.
St. Louis:
  Mrs. Arthur B. Baer, 9425 Ladue Road, St. Louis Co., Mo.
California:
  Mrs. Spencer Thorpe, 339 South Kingsley Dr., Los Angeles, Cal.
New England:
  Mrs. John H. Cunningham, 53 Seaver Street, Brookline, Mass.
Western Reserve:
  Mrs. A. E. Boethelt, 5925 Corydon Rd., Clev. Hts., Ohio.
Portland, Oregon:
  Miss Arlie Seaman, 2755 S. W. Summit Drive, Portland, Ore.

Saw Mill Farm
New City, New York

•

HERBRIETIES
Reg. U. S. Pat. Off.

We make a wonderful Mustard.
We call it
HONEY MUSTARD

We make
SALAD BLESSING—
All its name implies

We make
MINTED APPLE CHUTNEY
Of intriguing texture and flavor

We make
GOLDEN GLOW
Its a sweet surprise

We make many other unique
Herb-flavored products

Available in fine stores
throughout the United States
or direct from

Saw Mill Farm
New City, Rockland County
New York

F. & F. Nurseries
SPRINGFIELD, NEW JERSEY

*A
Wide
Selection
of
Perennial
Herb Plants*

•

CATALOG

Vigorous Herb Plants in Many Varieties

**SCENTED and OLD FASHIONED
COLORED-LEAVED
GERANIUMS
A SPECIALTY**

Price List on Request

VILLAGE HILL NURSERY
WILLIAMSBURG, MASS.

The Country Store

F. H TRUMBULL, Prop.

1 Monument St.,   Concord, Mass^tts

John M. Wagner
             Herbs and Spices

House of Herbs Products

*All types of
General Merchandise
from Penny Candies to
Smart Sportswear*

Catalogue Upon Request

HERBS

FROM

THE LITTLE HOUSE

ANNISQUAM, MASS.

HERBS

In addition to the popular herbs in small containers purchasable separately, we offer attractive assortments as follows. Mail orders filled.

No. 300 Seasoning and
   Herb Set $3.00
   Assorted herbs and vinegars

Flavor Foursome Set   2.75
   Four 4½ oz. jars of assorted
   herbs

Griffith's Spice Set   3.50
   12 jars of spices in a cabinet

Griffith's Kit of Spices   1.34
   Six jars of assorted spices and
   seasonings

Vinegar Adventures Set   2.50
   Four 8 oz. bottles of assorted
   flavored vinegars

Hanging Shelf of Herbs
   and Seasonings   3.60
   10 small jars of herbs and shelf

S. S. PIERCE CO.
133 Brookline Avenue
Boston

WEATHERED OAK HERB FARM
BRADLEY BOULEVARD   Charles H. Merryman, Manager   **BETHESDA 14, MARYLAND**

Owing to drastic conditions, many changes have been made so that the high quality of our products may remain the same.

DRIED HERBS: Intriguing blends for Salads, Omelets, Soups, Poultry Stuffing, Tomato Recipes, Stews, Sauces, Seafood, Etc.

HERB COOKERY: Attractive booklet containing excellent herb recipes. Sent on receipt of 25 cents.

Latest catalogue 10 cents

Culinary-dried herb combinations
Herb Vinegars
Horehound Candy

SHERMAN K. and **VERA B. HARDY**
EIGHTY HILL STREET   LEXINGTON, MASS.
ORIGINATORS *of the* HERB-BAR

Second Printing

Herbs

How to Grow Them and How to Use Them

By **HELEN NOYES WEBSTER**

Complete — Practical — Low Priced

Here you will find famous plans of herb gardens: lists for planting period gardens and for herb families; the herbs to use in modern gardens; valuable information about the use of herbs: and of course complete cultural information. Written by one of the country's leading authorities, it will make it easy to have an herb garden that will be a delight to you and the envy of your friends.

160 pages---36 illustrations, Octavo only, $1.50.   Postpaid in U. S.
Make checks payable to

HORTICULTURE, Horticultural Hall, Boston, Mass.

www.ingramcontent.com/pod-product-compliance
Lightning Source LLC
LaVergne TN
LVHW051113080426
835510LV00018B/2017